Chapter One

A Past-Life Memory

I don't know just how long ago the first time the feeling came to me, or just exactly where I was, but I was driving my car. I had seen a white cinderblock building that triggered an emotion that I could not describe. This same emotion came to me again, many months later, when I noticed another white cinderblock building. The feeling haunted and perplexed me.

I stopped at a light in the left-turn lane, when somewhere from within my mind's caverns came a mental vision of me with my mother, now deceased. Just a vision. Not much more.

We were standing in front of a two-story building. She and I both wore coats, and she had a scarf on her head in the form of a babushka. Maybe I wore one too, but I don't remember. I probably did. The air must have had a slight chill, but not uncomfortably so. My Aunt Miriam, my mother's sister, stood with us.

We stood there, between the building and the curb, if there was a curb, with my mother holding my hand. I was probably about seven or eight years old. There were other people standing outside this building as well. Many people. Just standing, waiting.

The building was white, and had five or six windows across both stories. The windows were long and narrow and fairly close together. I felt that it might be an apartment building.

I cannot picture a door, but I feel that my mother and I came out of that building from the rear. We had followed my Aunt Miriam, and I remember the shuffling of our feet as we walked through a dark corridor to a narrow staircase that descended to the outside world. The flooring was made of wood or concrete, and the walk was, to a small child, a long way.

We stood waiting at the front of this building. For what, I didn't know. For my father to come home? I'm not sure. It was a long wait, what felt like more than an hour or maybe even two. Did he finally show? I don't know, but I feel as though he did.

The building, although having only five or six windows across, took up what seemed like a city block. At least it was the only building on that plot of land. I remember seeing streets on three sides of the building. They were not paved, so there probably were no curbs. The streets were sand-colored and dusty with fine little stones. There were no automobiles. There was sunshine, like that of a late fall day.

Why I had this vision, or what there was about a white cinderblock building that provoked it, I'm not sure, but I did not forget it. It stuck in my mind for many months without a reason or connection to anything in my life. It was not until many months had passed, perhaps even more than a year, that this vision came back into my mind again plaguing me with its questions.

Chapter Two

An Unusual Haunting Feeling

I was driving along and my eyes gazed upon a white cinderblock house. Its windows could have been long and narrow like the ones in my former vision, or not. I don't remember.

What I do remember is how the sight of that house grabbed at my heart and at my emotions. Something haunted me and something inside me ached. It was all very puzzling. I kept driving. And at some point, the vision of the white building where my mother and I had stood outside reappeared in my mind.

I dismissed the experience. I told no one of the unusual haunting feeling, and I forgot about it for many months to come.

Some time later, the experience repeated itself. This time I was driving along as before, casually taking in the sites on either side of the road. It was a somewhat rural but local area. Some of the homes were bricked, while others were sided. Perhaps some were even log cabins that had been covered with a new facade. Suddenly, another white cinderblock home appeared, and again something vast pulled at my heart without my understanding why.

Now I mentioned it to a couple of my closest friends, and each listened without offering much comment. I again dismissed my thoughts, but did not put them away so far back in my memory. I wanted to know why I felt that way when I saw a white cinderblock building.

I began consciously looking for other cinderblock buildings and homes. When I was enroute somewhere that had open land, or a mix of home styles and structures, I studied them carefully to find out more. Matt, my gentleman friend, had told me that early settlers placed their homes by waterways; that would be where I might find older, less contemporary homes.

The next building that pulled at my emotions was a stable, and it, too, was white and cinderblock. It had long, narrow openings for the horses. It also brought the same gasping emotion and tugged at my heartstrings. What was it that was doing that to me? Where in my memory had some experience been planted so deeply to haunt me and draw such a profound reaction?

Chapter Three

In My Travels

The regiment of my workweek was getting such that a break was in order.   Even though a four-day Easter holiday weekend was coming close, an invitation to join in on a business trip with my friend, Gwenn, came at a good time.   She was always great company and her lively chatter kept us both in good spirits.

Gwenn was traveling to Dayton, Ohio, and I agreed to accompany her. This would give us the ride there and back to converse, shop, and have dinner together.

I sat in the conference room while Gwenn conducted her meeting. Her brunette hair shone brightly from the sun coming into the window. She spoke with firm authority and knowledge, and her colleagues warmly received her manner of presentation.

I read some material that I had brought with me, and did not concern myself with her business or she with mine. The meeting ended shortly after 5:00 p.m., and then we were free to enjoy the rest of the evening.

We went shopping at a half-off bookstore. I noted to myself that I had no interest in any type of mystery, and psychic phenomena offered no intrigue.   Yet, I was experiencing both. We then went to dinner and soon to sleep having spent a full day.

On our trip home, the plan was to take back roads rather than the main highway and to do some venturing. We wanted to spend our time stopping in small towns to shop, to see the countryside, and a change of scenery.

I found a flea market, which was a favorite shopping ground for me. I loved bargain hunting for inexpensive treasures. Gwenn found a craft store and an art store which pleased her. We had lunch in the area and then went on making our way through the towns.

Remembering my unsolved mystery, she mentioned that I should keep my eye out for houses or buildings that triggered this strange response.

We looked at a map before continuing our journey. We found an area called Ghost Town and thought it would be fun to take the route that would get us there. While the ghost town offered no intrigue, en route we came upon a municipal office building that was both white and cinderblock. We could see that the building was closed, and we parked in front on the street.

The emotions evoked by this building were mild, but there, nonetheless. I got out of the car and went up to the building to see if anything could be learned from this visit.

I looked through the windows. In a very few moments, I got some very distinct messages of yes or no, and mostly no, when I peered at furniture and other furnishings in the room.

The first object that I saw was a wooden chair, and I studied this chair. It had no seat covering and was a Country or Early American style. My mind said yes to the wooden chair, no to the style, and no to the light color of wood.

I gazed around the room seeing a desk, a file cabinet, and an orange shag rug on the floor. Each object said no, too new. Against the wall was an electric heater similar to one my grandmother had inside a basement fireplace, and again my mind said no, too new.

Both windows that I peered through were covered with cobwebs. And at each window my answer was that there were no cobwebs in my building's windows. Not maybe, but no cobwebs. For whatever reason, I was getting definite messages. Answers.

I walked back to the car and reported my findings. "Gwenn," I said, "how strange. I got yes or no answers, all very quickly. Mostly no, but I feel sure about the answers. There was no question as to how I related to each object in the building, and mostly no, not right, but I definitely determined a relationship."

I was intrigued. The only thing in that room that I identified with was a wooden chair, and it wasn't the right chair. But I knew it.

Gwenn was just as amazed with my reaction to this building and its contents. With little to go on we traveled on, laughing and talking about many things unrelated to this mind-boggling event; however, we both kept a watchful eye for other buildings to bring more reactions and answers. We knew that we were not even close to solving this mystery, but it was clear to me that she had an interest.

Chapter Four

The Discovery
(First Dialog)

Our trip continued toward home, and we now approached the point where our side trip met up with an appropriate point to get back onto the main highway. As we rode along, we discussed the strange experience that I had and the answers that told me almost nothing, just what was not right.

"The chair was right," I said, "but the wrong style. Wood was right, but the wrong color of wood. My chair was dark, very, very dark wood. And it had straight lines, not Country or Early American."

"How about the back; did it have spindles?" Gwenn asked.

"No, no round spindles; straight lines."

"How about the rungs of the chair; were they round?"

"No, straight," I said.

She then asked me, "Can you picture the room where the chair sits that you feel is right?"

"No, I don't think so," I replied. "Well, maybe."

She continued. "Is there a window in that room?"

"Yes," mentally picturing a window.

Simultaneously with her asking, "Are there window-panes?" thin lines of wood forming large squares appeared in the windows that I envisioned.

"Yes," I replied.

Flashes of dark and white windowpanes entered my mind. Were they there, were they white like the white building I saw or dark like the dark chair? I didn't know. I wasn't even sure now that there were small windowpanes.

"I'm not sure, Gwenn. I don't know if your suggestion made me see those windowpanes."

"Okay," she said. "Is there a bed in this room?"

"Yes," I replied.

"Is it a single bed?"

Without hesitation I answered "No, double."

"Oh, you know it's a double bed," she remarked. "Interesting."

"Was there a quilt on that bed?"

Again, without the time to reflect, I was speaking because the vision was already there. "Yes, a white quilt, with lots of stitches. It was machine stitched, not hand stitched, and it has some small patches of color in it."

She continued. "Can you see above the bed?"

"I don't know." A blurry vision was trying to make it through. "Yes," I said. "I think so."

"Is there anything on the wall above the bed?"

Questioningly I said, "Maybe . . . maybe a picture."

"What's in that picture? Can you see it?"

"Maybe some flowers. In flowerpots. Soft colors."

"What's the frame like on that picture. Is it brass?"

"No, it's gold. I think it's gold." Now I wasn't sure if my mind was seeing a more recent picture. "The picture is too new, and the frame is too gold. It's polished brass," I said.

"I'm not sure, Gwenn. I may be imagining this picture and the frame. I'm not sure about the gold. It's too bright."

"Can you see the floor of this room?" she continued.

"Yes, it's wood."

"Like mine?" she asked.

"Wood, like yours, but dark wood. Not polished."

"Are there marks in the wood?"

"Yes, dark marks. The wood is unfinished with dark marks. Very old, distressed wood."

Now we both knew that she had the ability to ask me questions about what was somewhere deep in my mind, and I could somehow see a vision and respond to what she was asking.

Somewhat alarmed I said, "This is too strange, Gwenn. I am speaking before even thinking. I don't know where these words are coming from. I'm just answering you.

It's as if I'm really there telling you what I see, and I'm not even sure this is real."

"It would be interesting to see what a hypnotist could find out from you."

"I'm responding as if in a hypnotic state."

"I find it really interesting that I can make you see these things and you are able to tell me what you see. I think we've got something here."

"I'm really freaked over this experience," I said. "Where have I been pulling this information from? What does it mean?"

We laughed, both amazed at the experience. As we rode along, we talked about other things to distract us; but our minds returned to the strangeness of how we both felt about this phenomenon and of being able to relate in this strange way.

Gwenn started again. "Let's try this," she said. "Is there a dresser in this room?"

Hesitantly I answered, "Yes, I think so. Maybe. It's dark wood, and has a rounded top."

"Can you see on top of the dresser? Is there a mirror and comb?"

"No. It's not a dresser. It's a chest of drawers. Maybe it has a mirror or comb, I can't tell."

"Is it maybe a bureau? Does that feel more comfortable?"

"No," I said.

"Can you see anything on the chest of drawers?"

"I think so. A scarf. A picture. There's a picture of my father."

"Are you sure it's your father?"

"Yes."

"How old is your father?"

"He's forty. And he's wearing a dark suit. Wide lapels. Very wide lapels."

"What else is on the chest of drawers?"

"Bottles. Little bottles. Glass. Like little colored, cut-glass perfume bottles."

"Is there a mirror in this room?"

"No. I can't see a mirror."

"Is there a closet in this room?"

"Yes."

"Can you see in this closet?"

Again, "Yes."

"What can you see?"

"Suits. Men's suits."

"How many?"

"Two or three."

"Anything else? Women's clothing?"

"Yes, dresses."

"How many dresses?"

"Four or five, maybe."

"What are they like? Are they cotton?"

"No, they're not cotton. They're more dressy."

"What material? What colors?"

"Silky. Bright colors, maybe a navy, one maybe flowered."

"How about the suits? What color are they?"

"One is blue, like a medium blue."

"Medium blue?"

"Like Brooks Brothers, a soft blue."

More conversation took place. We talked about the peculiarities of what I was finding, and she continued asking what else was in this closet.

"Is there a shelf in the closet?"

"Yes."

"What's on the shelf?"

"Boxes."

"Boxes? What kind of boxes?"

"I don't know. Shoe boxes, maybe," now laughing because of my own closets at home which had all of my many shoes in boxes on the closet shelf.

"What else is on that shelf?"

Questioningly, I answered "A hat?" not knowing if I saw a hat or not.

"What kind of hat?"

"A ladies hat."

"Like the kind you would wear to church?"

"No, a wide-brimmed hat."

"Well, that would seem to fit the era we're looking at," she said.

She didn't ask, but I pictured the hat to be navy blue with a white flower attached.

"Now let's look at the floor of the closet. What's on the floor?"

"Shoes," I replied.

"Ladies shoes?"

"Yes."

"How many?"

"Two pair, maybe."

"What are they like?"

"Clunky . . . you know. Wide heels."

"How wide?"

"Like this," I said, showing her a finger span of about three quarters of an inch. "Wide."

"How about the front? Open?"

"Maybe. Definitely not a pump. Maybe crossed straps, probably open toe, with some kind of a strap. Wide strap."

The trip progressed with more dialog. Each time I was questioningly responding from a memory, somewhere from within, sometime in my lifetime or past lifetime, I didn't know.

"What era do you think we're looking at?" I asked.

"I'm thinking we're looking at some time in the twenties, don't you think?" she said. "The dark wood, the clothing. Sounds like about the twenties."

"I wouldn't know. I'm not any good at knowing time periods. I've never had an interest in old things or history."

I also knew that I would now be interested, and my pursuit for answers would make my idle mind inquisitive in regard to things that would give me answers.

"Gwenn," I said, "I feel this couldn't have taken place in my current lifetime. I'm about ten years old, and my father is 40. My father was 40 when he married my mother. Maybe it's an old picture, but I don't feel that it is."

"Is your father in the house?" she asked.

"No. He's away."

"Away," she said. "He's not living there now?"

"No. He's away. He's coming back, but he's not here now."

"How about your mother; is she there?"

"Yes, she's there."

"Okay, let's try this. Do you hear anything?"

"No."

"Can you smell anything?"

"No."

"But you feel your mother is there in the house?"

"Yes."

"How do you know?   Can you hear her?"

"Yes."

"What do you hear?"

"I hear a broom, maybe."

"Is she talking?"

"No, I don't think so. Maybe."

"Do you hear anything else?"

"Maybe a radio."

Gwenn said, "I think we're on a wavelength here. Somehow I am able to pull this information from you."

This was all very interesting and very perplexing. Where was all of this coming from?

"Let's try this," she said. "Let's take you outside of that room. Can you walk through the doorway into another part of the house?"

I tried. "No," I said. "Something is pulling me back."

"Like what?" she asked.

"I don't know. Like big rubber bands pulling me back. They won't let me out of the room."

"Okay, let's look at the room you are in. Can you see out the window?"

"I don't know. I think I see green, like grass and trees, but I don't know what window I'm looking out of. It could be one I remember from the house I was raised in. Probably is."

Again, "Is there a mirror in this room?"

"No," giving time to mentally scan the room. "I can't find a mirror."

"Okay. Look around the room. Is there anything else you can see?"

"I don't think so. I think we've pulled about all we can from this experience, don't you?"

"Maybe. But I think it's really fascinating that I can draw that information from you just by asking questions."

Again our conversation drifted on to other things and then back to this new means of discovery.

She pursued some more. "Can you see the bottom of the chest of drawers?"

"Yes."

"Are there legs or is it sitting on the floor?"

"There are legs. High legs."

"What's under there?"

"Dust!" I replied, seeing large balls of dust in my mind's eye, and knowing how easily dust accumulates on hardwood floors.

She laughed, thinking "of course."

"What's under the bed?" she continued.

IMMEDIATE RESPONSE, laughing, and with a true shudder, "I don't want to look under the bed."

We both laughed, but I knew that I did not want to look under that bed. It terrified me.

By this time we were both thirsty and decided to pull off of the road and stop for an ice-cold pop.

Still laughing about my not wanting to look under the bed she asked, "What do you suppose is under the bed that you don't want to see?"

"I don't know, and I hate to even tell you what I'm feeling."

"What's that?"

"I feel like it's a body, or an arm and hand moving. What if I was molested as a small child? Maybe it's a furry animal, like a stuffed animal, human like, or maybe like a monkey or ape with claws. Something with claws. Maybe it's no more than a stuffed animal that frightened me as a child and I've hidden it under the bed. I kind of feel that it's a child's fear. But I don't want to look under that bed!" Then I laughed.

We finished our drinks and got back into the car. We rode along, laughing and talking about many things. Then I spotted another white cinderblock building off of the highway with a railroad track running in front of it.

"Gwenn, see that building over there? That is something like the building I saw in my first vision. It is two story and has about the same number of windows at each level."

"Oh, so we have to find a building with a train track running in front of it?" she asked.

"No, no train track. But that building is like what I saw."

We both began to reflect on the good time we were having and what an outsider might think about our experience. We laughed about trying to explain our trip to others. In fact, I made jokes of the trip I had just had to some other part of my life, current or past.

Gwenn said, "Yes, we had one trip to Dayton," and I finished the statement.

"And one to Chicago."

"Chicago?" Gwenn questioned.

Now where did that come from? Was my memory of that last white building with the train track in Chicago? Or was there something about a train and Chicago? That seemed to make sense. Why Chicago? Why did I say that?

I professed to ask my Aunt Addie if my father or I had ever been to Chicago. To her knowledge, we had not.

"Let's try to get you outside of that room another way," she said. "Try backing out of the room."

"Okay. It's not working. I'm in your house. I see your hallway and your doors. It's your color of wood, so I know it's your house." Her doors had an inset of a reddish tone stain, widely bordered in white.

"Can you see anything else in the room besides the bed, the chair, and the chest of drawers?"

Thoughtfully, my mind again perused the room. I could only see the objects that we had identified. I shook my head and said "No."

"Can you open the drawers of the chest?" she asked.

I mentally tried. I could not. "No," I said.

"Can you sit on the floor?"

"Yes."

"Okay, sit on the floor."

"All right."

"Can you look under the bed?"

"I don't want to look under the bed!" I chuckled. I did not want to look under that bed. We both laughed.

"Is there molding at the base of the wall?"

"Yes."

"What is it like?"

"Wood. Dark wood."

"Let's try this. Walk to the door of the room and stand at the doorway."

"Okay."

"Now, put your hand on the doorframe and walk outside of the room."

"I can't. I keep ending up in your house."

"Can you feel the doorframe?"

"Yes."

"What's it like?"

"Wood; layered wood."

"Can you reach beyond the doorframe?"

"I can touch the wall. It's rough."

"Is it wallpapered?"

"No. Rough."

"Like stucco?"

"No. Its rough paint. Was paint rough years ago?" I asked.

"Yes. Sometimes plaster was even swirled."

I countered, "Yes, my girlfriend Margo's house has that swirled rough-textured plaster, but her walls are stained, not painted. But the wall I just touched was just a rough-textured painted wall."

Approaching Toledo, at about the halfway point to home, Gwenn asked, "Do you feel like doing something spontaneous?"

She nor I rarely did anything spontaneous. We were both set planners, very deliberate and well disciplined. If it wasn't in the plan, it usually didn't happen. We laughed about our inability to deviate from our stringency, and agreed we should loosen up and enjoy more freedom.

Since I had no plan other than this trip, it was easy for me to follow along and say yes. We veered off of the highway at the Toledo exit. Gwenn was speaking out loud to herself, but I couldn't understand what she was saying. She soon started to cut down side streets into a neighborhood that I did not know, or know where she was headed.

She pulled up in front of a house and said, "That's the house, and the door is open. Let's go in. This is a lady that was married to my late father's cousin."

As we approached the house, the door opened. A lady about our age walked out and explained that she was going to work, but that her mother was inside.

We entered and found Josephine sitting on the couch welcoming us to sit down. She was a fairly large woman with white hair and a pleasant smile. Her cane rested on the couch beside her.

She was quite friendly, and we chatted awhile. She and Gwenn talked mostly about family members and their current status. Josephine spoke of her interest in singing karaoke with friends and invited us to join her that evening. She recommended that we have dinner at the restaurant that had karaoke. We could eat around 7:00 p.m. and karaoke would begin at nine o'clock.

I never thought Gwenn would be interested, but her need for spontaneity was ruling. She asked me, "Would you feel like doing that?"

I replied that it would be fine.

I observed the walls of this old house. They were the rough, textured paint like I had felt earlier in my mental vision. I later learned that the house was a hundred years old. I studied other parts of the house: the archways, the tile in the bathroom, the fixtures, and so on. Nothing triggered any further information for my puzzle.

Josephine asked if we would like to play cards before going to dinner. Gwenn said yes, but soon said she would really like to look at her family pictures if she had any.

"Yes, of course," Josephine replied. With that we accompanied her downstairs to the basement and brought up the old pictures.

Gwenn was satisfying a need to identify with family ties and fulfilling a promise to stop in on one of her trips past Toledo. I didn't know it, but she was also on a quest to solve my mystery. With a dual cause in mind, she wanted to find out if anything in that old house or the contents of the pictures gave me any further clues as to missing pieces of my puzzle.

The pictures contained many of Gwenn's and Josephine's family members enjoying themselves at family gatherings. I saw ladies with similar shoes to what was in my closet, and a lady with a wide-brimmed hat like the one on my shelf.

We put the pictures away, resolved to have dinner at the recommended restaurant, and then to enjoy karaoke. At 1:30 in the morning, I pulled into my driveway, went into the house, and to bed.

The next day I heard trains and train whistles in my head.

Chapter Five

Another Day of Travel

Another day of travel with Gwenn, only this trip was for pleasure and we had a plan. We were in search of a flea market to browse in, as was suggested by some friends, and we set off for Imlay City.

Taking back roads to make our journey more interesting, we looked for white, cinderblock buildings that might give me another side journey into my past.

Before departing on our one-day trip, I spoke to Gwenn about having a fear of what I might find out.

"What if my mind takes me some place that I don't want to go, or I can't come back?" I said.

"We should talk about setting up safety nets for you so that you are comfortable," she stated.

"Like what?" I asked.

"You have to feel that when you travel into some unknown place and feel that you don't like it, are afraid or uncomfortable, that I can pull you back to safety."

"How would you do that?" I inquired.

"You would have to feel that you were holding my hand, and if you reached a point that you didn't want to explore or you were frightened, you could let me know and I would pull you to safety."

"I do trust you, so I think that would work."

Not one building pulled at my heart strings the way some others had. I rationalized that my building must be a house that looked lived in rather than an empty building, and certainly not a cinderblock barn or warehouse like many we had seen that day.

However, we did come upon an empty building meeting the qualifications of white and cinderblock, and parked the car. I had brought a camera along just in case I found a building that moved me in some mysterious way; I could then capture it on film to look at later.

There was a house nearby with a car parked outside. The empty building was probably on the same property as the lived-in house, and most likely belonged to the people that lived there.

I sat in the car looking at the building, peering at the broken window, two open doorways, and the darkness inside. Gwenn was silent, allowing my mind to run freely.

"Gwenn," I said, "the strangest thing is happening. My mind wants to go back in time. It is *leaping* back in time. Traveling back. It wants to go back so badly, but I'm not finding anything. I can feel it racing backwards."

"You're traveling back in time, are you?"

"Yes, leaping back in time."

I let time pass.

I resolved to get out of the car and go up to the empty building. I stood at the open doorway on the right and peered inside. I looked directly into the basement. There were no stairs, and my mind said, "No basement."

I looked at the second open doorway to the left and peered inside. I could see a door lying angled on the floor and somewhat leaning on its side in the middle of this small room. Broken glass from the window was also on the floor. I could see laundry tubs, a washing machine, and what looked like a shower stall on the main floor in the room beyond.

There was another small room to the right of the back room, but I couldn't tell what was in it. It was fairly light in there from the windows, and not particularly scary, but I didn't want to go inside. I was afraid, but not afraid of what I would see. I was afraid of where my mind would take me.

I went back to the car to think about it, and told Gwenn how I felt. I said that I would go in, but that I had to build up the courage. I was afraid. I described what I could see and that nothing was particularly frightening; yet, I was afraid to go in.

She asked if I would be more comfortable if she walked up to the building with me, and I told her yes.

She grabbed my camera and we walked up to the building. She hung back long enough to take my picture in front of the building and accompanied me to the doorway.

I walked inside, carefully stepping around the door on the floor and the broken glass. I looked back to see if Gwenn was still visible before I peered into the back rooms, both containing large showers. Her presence comforted me, but she did not come into the building. The floor was made of a concrete block, as well as its walls, but I did not relate to it as having any special meaning; it had no significance to me.

A second older washing machine was in the back room to the right with the second shower. A wooden table of dark wood was in the shower room to the left. No other objects were in the rooms, and I related to nothing. I experienced no emotional sensitivity.

We got back into the car and discussed what the building may have been used for. There was an orchard across the road, and we decided that it was a building for the workers of the orchard to shower in and have their clothing washed. Gwenn thought perhaps there was a ladies and men's shower, and that each had their own washing machine.

Again we set off looking for the type of white cinderblock building that aroused my psyche. As we rode along, Gwenn talked about some encounters she had witnessed through her psychology training in becoming a police officer in an earlier career.

She told me of many things about which I had no experience. I would not have believed many of them except that Gwenn was so totally logic-driven. She related to having first-hand knowledge of mind-energy experiences that worked. She reported of someone being able to take a picture of something, like a table in a dining room of a house; and, when the film was developed, the people who used to live there were visibly sitting at the table. I found this impossible to believe, although my own experiences were just as unbelievable.

I later found a woman who had such a gift. She shot numerous photographs where objects or entities would show up on film but could not be seen by others who accompanied her.

Gwenn related another experience of being able to form together as a group and to create enough energy to lift a 250-pound person using two fingers each. I tended to disbelieve her again. She continued telling me of more events, but I questioned her.

"You mean you actually, as a group, put your hands on a table and mentally made that table rise?" I asked. "Like the theory of an energy moving the hand piece on a Ouija board?"

"Yes, that actually happened," she proclaimed. I was now slightly believing in this personality which was so much like my own . . . honest, logical, and non-exaggerating. Yet, I was not totally convinced. I questioned, doubted and believed, all at the same time. Could this really be?

We continued our philosophical conversation. I spoke about my fear of traveling into some unknown area of my mind and finding something I did not want to find.

"I'm afraid of maybe finding out something I won't like. Maybe there was molestation somewhere in my past."

"Molestation?" she asked.

"I say that because of what I first felt was under the bed, but I don't know. It could have been a stuffed animal that we talked about or some other child's fear. I would like to feel it was a child's fear, but I first thought I saw a moving arm and hand."

"Did you feel that you were pushed under the bed?" she asked.

"It would be more like pulled, wouldn't it?" I questioned.

"Is that what you felt? Consider this," she said. "Could it be that you were told that the boogie man lived under the bed?"

"Yes, that could be," I conceded. "That would be a logical child's fear."

I digressed back in thought. "What makes you think that you could pull me back to safety and not travel with me?" I asked. "You are so in tune with me; what makes you think you could stop from going with me?"

Now I thought I had posed a potential problem to her.

"No," she said flatly. "I'm not feeling what you're feeling, and my feet are going to be planted firmly on the ground. I will protect you, and the sound of my voice and the feel of my hand will pull you to safety."

Still unsure and unconvinced, I continued. "Are you sure that you could keep from traveling with me, and that you could stop it if you were part of my past life?"

"If I found that I was part of your past life or vision, I would not go with you. I would pull you back and then we would talk about it. I would not go with you and leave you unprotected."

I felt more assured.

Chapter Six

Graveyard Walk

The day continued. As we rode along, we came upon a cemetery. My mind had drifted off.

I recalled a strange experience that had happened in my life while I was going through a divorce about six years' prior. I surmised that all of these things were pieces of a puzzle that began to surface at about the same time . . . the vision of the two-story white building with my mother and I standing outside in front; the white cinderblock buildings pulling at my heart the way they did; and the video-type visions that I had, one of which included a spirit and the presentation of three tombstones.

This particular night I had fallen asleep and wanted to wake up, but could not pull myself out of that sleep. My gentleman friend, Matt, was present. I fought to wake up, but couldn't. It was so frightening. I couldn't break out of that sleep. I eventually did, but I was panic-stricken. I related my fight to awaken myself to Matt, who understood. He at one time had also experienced that horrible fight to wake up.

That same night, still trying to catch some strained sleep, I had three slow-motion visions that became close up, paused, and then went on. The visions seemed unrelated.

The first was of a lady with dark skin. Her smile was as broad as her face. The vision of her was in slow motion. Then a close-up view zoomed in and held on her pleasant expression. It was a bright day, and she wore something on her head like a headdress. It was difficult to see the headpiece as only small fragments of color were visible against her dark hair. She was smiling ever so sweetly.

The motion picture continued. Galloping horses. White galloping horses came into view. That was the second vision. Did the dark-skinned lady with the headdress tie in with the white galloping horses? Was she Indian and perhaps those were the horses of the Indians in my past?

Since then, I found a greeting card with a picture of an Indian lady with a broad smile and rosy cheeks very much like the lady in the dreamlike vision. I have also seen pictures of Indians with white horses. I had some Indian heritage, which made me wonder if this was due to some akashic memory.

Again I continued my restless sleep, and the dreamlike images appeared before my closed eyes. The third vision took place in a graveyard. Round-topped tombstones stood before me. I seemed to be walking through the cemetery. I stopped and stared as a ghost-like figure sprung from behind the tombstones. It moved briskly from place to place and then disappeared.

Suddenly, light appeared. A stream of illuminating light ran across the tops of two of the tombstones. It moved from one side of the rounded top to the other, one at a time, like a fluorescent tube. These two grave markers were placed relatively close to one another. My eyes followed the brilliant, illuminating light through a path of many grave stones until it stopped at the third one to point it out with the same demonstration. The vision was then over and I was startled and fully awake. I was aware of having an extremely heightened sense.

It occurs to me now that all of these supernatural events have taken place since the death of my mother, which was about ten years ago. She is the tie that I have to the Indian heritage, for it was her mother's ancestry that was from the Crow Indian tribe.

The illuminating light was to point something out to me, I am sure. It was to say something, to make something known. What, I do not know, but I sense it is something about my ancestry.

My personal theory is that one is reincarnated from their own heritage; that is, I believe that I probably lived as an Indian at some time, and in Croatia, where my father's ancestors were from in another incarnation.

I looked for information on the Crow Indian tribe and found that it was formed over a 300-year period. The Crow Indians lived mostly in Wyoming and Nebraska. I found that in old folklore, it was believed that the crow signaled death. In Indian lore, however, I found that the crow represented a messenger who would call us home or warn of change.

For whatever reason, approaching the cemetery, Gwenn asked me, "Do you have any interest? Should I pull in?"

I reflected back on my vision of the tombstones in the cemetery and said yes. She pointed out a round-topped grave marker, and I said to her, "No, too thick. The tombstones I saw were much thinner."

Gwenn immediately cued in on the fact that these graves were too recent and we needed to go to an older part of the cemetery. She pointed to a nearby gravestone, and then another, asking if they were more like the ones that I had seen in my vision.

I said yes because of their rounded-tops, but explained that they had been larger in my vision. That I knew. I got out of the car and went up to one of the grave markers. I studied it. I went on to the next and again stared at its size and shape, the inscription, and the year of death. I looked at another and another, taking in the information I could glean from them.

I got back into the car. "They were all from the early 1800's," I exclaimed. "Most were about 1825, and some I couldn't even read."

"That's earlier than we thought, isn't it?" she asked.

"Yes, it is. I wonder if the year is connected with the visions I have had and the other things that I am feeling and experiencing."

"Maybe. Maybe not," she said.

We left the cemetery, and as we rode along we passed many white cinderblock barns and other block buildings. I felt no identification with any of them.

We continued on with our journey, now approaching Port Huron through the back roads. There was a store there that we were heading for, but it would be evening soon. The decision to explore the area in daylight prevailed, and our quest went on.

We came upon another cemetery, and again Gwenn asked the question of whether or not I wanted to go in.

"Yes, I do," I said. "I want to check out the years on the markers that are similar to those that I saw earlier."

We entered, went directly to the older part of the cemetery, and Gwenn began to point out the grave markers that she was seeing.

I got out of the car and began to walk. Each marker that I studied in this area was from around 1865. That was the birth date era; the death dates were around 1920. Now it was beginning to tie in. Maybe there was some connecting thread.

I went back to the car and explained my findings to Gwenn. 1920 was the time frame in which she thought the room with the wooden chair and bed had been. She comprehended. "There may be a tie after all," she said.

Chapter Seven

A Psychic's Perspective

On several occasions I have taken the opportunity to see a tarot card reader. I was usually accompanied by one or more friends, or sometimes by my Aunt Addie.

Aunt Addie was a cute little woman with dark curly hair, and she continually looked for information regarding a lost love. Sometimes she would ask about her son's health as he had suffered with back problems even after his surgery.

After a reading, we would compare notes and wonder if the things projected would ever come true. For myself, surely some things were of amazing resemblance of facts of my character and surroundings, friends and family. The future predictions left me with great intrigue and anticipation. Months later, things predicted could be tied to occurrences in my life.

On one particular day at a psychic fair, I saw a lady who seemed to tell me things of little or no consequence to my life. I felt that she was not at all able to connect to me spiritually. Of particular note was the comment about my daughter's life not having anything extraordinary in it when she had recently been engaged to be married.

Feeling disappointed, and already having agreed to pay a fee for this service, I asked her if she could read anything about past lives. She said that she could, and I related my experiences with white cinderblock buildings and the emotions that they evoked.

Her response was this. "You may have been left to die in a building such as that, and your death may not have been for a good reason. Maybe you were left behind and someone else was to pick you up, but that didn't happen. There was a mistake, and they thought that someone else was going to get you."

She suggested that the next time I came upon a building that brought about those feelings that I should stop. I should go up to the building and go inside if I could. Of course, it would have to be unoccupied to do this. She said doing this would bring back memories, and I would be able to recall clues as to what had happened to me.

Feeling nonplussed and disbelieving, I paid the lady her fee and gave little credibility to her comments. However, I felt that if the occasion ever arose to find such a building empty, I might try to approach it.

Sometime later I was traveling with Gwenn and she remembered what the psychic had said to me. We were on an almost desolate road. We were going up north when we found a small, vacant cinderblock building standing all alone and way back off of the road.

It was winter, and after many a snowfall for the season, I set off on foot through an open field. I was wearing 18 inch high boots, and went plunging through three feet of snow to get to this building. I wanted so much to see if it could bring answers to my mystery.

The building was cinderblock and it was empty. There was no glass where the windows should go and no door in the doorway. It also was not white, but a natural block, and did not evoke the emotions that some buildings of the past had done. It was worth a try, however, and my patient and interested friend was willing to give this venture due attention.

I approached the building feeling nothing. I walked all around. Still nothing. I went inside, saw an electrical cord where there once had been a light fixture, cobwebs at the windows, straw on the ground floor, and felt nothing. I trudged back to the car and reported that it offered no new information.

Chapter Eight

Enlightenment

"You know, Gwenn," I said one evening when we met for dinner, "I'm just beginning to figure out that I am probably remembering very small parts from many past lives."

"Oh?" she said. "What makes you say that?"

"Well, I feel that maybe I remember parts of four or five past lives. I feel that the life with the house, chair, and bed in the room is from one life, and the vision with my mother and I on the outside of the white building is another, and the white cinderblock building that haunts me is still another. Also, the dark-skinned lady and the white galloping horses may be from another lifetime. The horse stable that I react to fits in with that one, too. But, for whatever reason, I am remembering small fragments from each."

"That may well be," she said. "I think we should make a point of taking another day for venturing to see if we can find any more buildings that might trigger something for you."

"That could be fun," I said in agreement.

Upon returning home that evening and looking at my mail, I received a travel ad in with my frequent flyer envelope. It was for an enchanting Greek Isles tour. On the face of the folded pamphlet was a vividly clear picture of a pure white Greek Temple with a dome roof and overlooking blue waters. My eyes were affixed to this temple, and I knew that I had been there inside a similar building. I could emotionally go in, feel myself kneeling, and having a dark shawl over my head. I was among others, and I could hear the murmur of prayer.

A beautiful sunny day presented itself the next time Gwenn and I decided to take a day for an enjoyable ride. We drove through many of the east-side cities for the sole purpose of visiting old, white buildings known to evoke some deep, heart rendering and gnawing feelings.

I wanted to take pictures of these buildings for future viewing as Gwenn's thoughtful chatter was not always conducive to my need for deep concentration. I needed to meditate and allow my mind to explore these feelings; therefore, I thought pictures might provide a means for me to study them later, quietly, to see what I could learn of any past-life memories.

We managed to find and photograph three buildings and I took several shots from different angles. When the pictures were developed, I studied them carefully. The results were interesting, with one being quite informative, but the others rendered disheartening results. They were not what I had hoped for.

The first photograph was of airforce barracks which were located not far from my home. I could not drive on the base, so the pictures, unfortunately, were not close up enough to be of any value for my purposes.

The second building, with three different views, did evoke some memory. It related to the two-story white building in one of my visions. When I looked into the upstairs window of this picture, my mind saw my brunette mother, who was blonde in this life, dressed in a navy blue dress. At one point she sat on the bed to put her shoes on. Her shoes were a clunky style and not feminine, but with a two inch heel, about three quarters of an inch thick. My mother's expression was pleasant and she was happy. I was in the room with her, and was about eight years old. The feeling was comfortable.

The third building, unfortunately, photographed much better than it actually appeared and therefore lost all of its mystique. In the photograph, it appeared to be well kept, and with the sun shining through brilliantly colored foliage, a pleasant place to be. It did not match the eerie feelings that I got when I looked at it in plain view. In fact, in the photographs, it reminded me of a nice apartment my grandparents had rented in sunny Florida prior to their moving there.

Some other day I would tour the other half of the city where I knew another handful of this type of old, white building to exist. I would then try this photography exercise again.

I decided to relax for the evening and to read a good novel. I found a passage in the book which read, "The light over the door still burned . . ." In my mind's eye, I saw the interior of a home, where I had lived at some time, with real candles burning on the wall. I remember my grandmother's home on my father's side having lights on the walls, but they were electric. The vision in my mind's eye was prior to this time period and I was about five years old.

Chapter Nine

The Indian's Headdress

The last trip I recently took with Gwenn was business for her and pleasure for me. We were in our room, and I looked through the hotel-provided visitor's guide of current local events. I noted that a "White Owl Cultural Pow Wow" had taken place the previous month in a nearby park. "Too bad it isn't going on now," I said. "I might have learned something by attending."

What I did learn, however, was from the accompanying picture in this hotel book. The Indian had on a headdress which looked exactly like the feathered headdress that I had seen on the dark-skinned lady in my vision. Specifically, the feathers were dark at the base for the first 1 to 1-1/2 inches with white at the tips. In my mental vision, it was only the white that I could see clearly against the lady's dark hair. I now knew for sure that it was a headdress that I had seen. The spirit world was generally kind enough to follow up with answers of confirmation.

I wondered if there was a significance to the type of feather or color combination used by individual tribes.

Chapter Ten

Where They Lie

I had fallen asleep on the couch while watching television. I slept until about 1:30 in the morning, and awakened to find myself thinking about the specific size of the tombstones that I had seen in my hallucinative or dreamlike state.

From driving through local graveyards, I knew that the tombstones here in Michigan were not the same size as those that I perfectly remembered. Mine were wider than any that I had seen here, and were probably deeper than the older ones that resembled their shape. They were also narrower than the new granite stones that were similar in style. *My tombstones probably measured a little more than two feet wide, nearly four feet high, and about three inches deep.* I felt that my tombstones were located somewhere else, in some other country.

I recalled how the illuminated spiritual light ran over the rounded tops, one at a time, until it had pointed out all three. I felt that there was some significance for my being shown three and that they were not here. I felt that the spirit was very real, and that it was trying to tell me something in regard to the people who were buried in the three gravesites.

I picked myself up off of the couch, still thinking about the tombstones. I mentally asked where they might be. I was on my way to the bedroom when a word and the letters c-h-e-r-i-t came to me spiritually in relation to the tombstones. It was something to do with their placement, and in my sleepy state, I picked up a pen and pad of paper to write this down. I knew that I would not be able to recall this information in the morning. I wrote these words on the pad of paper and went to bed.

C-h-e-r-i-t, in relation to tombstones--placement?

I had never heard of the word, but its spelling was clearly given to me.

In the morning, while having my coffee in the kitchen, I recalled having written that note. I went back to the bedroom to get the small pad of paper on which I had scribbled. I then went to the bookshelf, pulled out the dictionary, and began to look for the word "cherit."

No such word was to be found, but I did find something very close and in my mind reasoned that in current-day English, a letter may have been dropped. What I found was chert, and its meaning was this:

> Chert: Any of various microscopic varieties
> of silica. A siliceous rock of chalcedonic or
> opaline silica occurring in limestone.
> Origin unknown.

The origin of the word may be unknown, but I knew that I must find out where chalcedonic or opaline silica limestone was prevalent.

Silica, I found through a small amount of research, has some interesting qualities. It is associated with health and longevity, and in some forms prevents cardiovascular and Alzheimer's disease.

I also learned that silica has qualities of protecting valuables from damage of moisture and damp air and acts as a natural dehumidifier. Porous silica is widely used as a packing material and its water is chemically bound in.

The word chalcedonic means some type of holder; anything from chains to a chair. A translation to chalice, a drinking cup, followed. Opaline, by definition, means to ooze.

I learned that black opals come from Australia and fire opals come from Mexico. Other precious opals of various colors come from Transylvania and Romania.

I felt that the tombstones might contain substances of silica or opaline, and found that there are manufacturers using these materials in North America. So far I've had no indication as to where either silica or opaline are prevalent or where the tombstones may lie.

Chapter Eleven

Ferdinand!

My daughter, Sue, had been recently widowed and was living with me. I hadn't been widowed, but I had been left alone after a fourteen-year relationship. We were both lacking male friends with whom to socialize.

Our mutual friend, Frank, whose age was between my age and Sue's, had called to ask if I would be interested in meeting one of his friends. Months earlier he had offered to introduce me to another friend who had recently divorced. Since that never materialized, I did not expect this meeting to transpire. However, I would wait for his confirming call that afternoon.

The afternoon call came, but to my surprise, Frank said that now both friends wanted to meet me at the same time. They were both my age, but I asked if Sue could come too, as I certainly did not want to be outnumbered with three men to one woman. We were all friends, so Frank said, "Of course." He liked Sue, too.

The five of us met for the evening. I particularly liked Frank's friend Frank, who was called Frank-O, to avoid the confusion of the two having the same name. The other fellow, Joe, was certainly a nice man, too.

Several weeks passed, and I didn't hear from either of them. When I talked to Frank I asked, "Didn't your friends like me?"

"Sure they did. I don't know why no one has called you. I'll see what's up."

Then one Sunday the telephone rang and it was Frank-O. He said that he and Joe had picked up some chicken and shrimp. He then asked if I would like them to come over and fix dinner. If I had a girlfriend to invite also, that would be fine, too.

"Great!" I responded. I called Mary, who was more than delighted to join us. I was surprised to find her available on short notice, but she was an unusually accommodating friend. She was nice to have around, and mixed well with my new friends.

Frank-O was quite attentive. He made a point to put his arm around me, hold my hand from time to time, and generally show interest. He even made a suggestion that maybe we would go over to the island on his boat the next weekend.

I was looking forward to the outing, but I never got a call all week or on the weekend. The friendship went on like that for over a year. Occasionally something would bring us together, we'd have a great time, but I never got a personal call or invitation. We would always be brought together by a group function.

"I'm going to be down at the boat all weekend; if you're not doing anything, why don't you and a girlfriend come on down," he would say. I would, weeks would pass, and nothing ever materialized between us.

Then, near Christmastime, I got a call from Joe. He said that he and Frank-O were going to have a Christmas party at his clubhouse, and he wanted to invite me to join them. I could bring a guest if I wanted.

Now I was really perplexed. Joe and Frank-O were so close that they could have been joined at the hip. Obviously, they had agreed that Joe was to call me; Frank-O did not want to extend a personal invitation. So, I boldly asked, "Is Frank-O bringing anyone?"

"I have no idea!" replied Joe. But rumor had it, I later learned from Frank, that a lot of Frank-O's old girlfriends would be there. He was going to show no partiality. So I decided that I would bring another gentleman friend to the party.

From that time on, Frank-O has been apprehensive, indifferent, and uncomfortable around me, and I around him. There is an undeniable attraction on both of our parts with basically no grounds.

Another year of this pretend friendship/relationship has taken place. Frank-O called once to come over and join me in the hot tub that I have outdoors, and once to go to breakfast under the pretense of wanting financial advice.

Each time he would come over, he would be fortified with a few beers for courage. He would dare to put his arm around me as if there was something going on between us. For whatever reason, I welcomed this small gesture of friendship based on no grounds. I really did not want a relationship with this man, but I could not explain what the apparent affinity was between us.

My daughter, Sue, established a closer friendship with Frank-O than myself, being friends with some of the younger people who rented rooms from Frank-O. She claimed that Frank-O was intimidated by me and that he certainly cared what I might think about him. She told me that sometimes Frank-O would remark, "Don't tell your mother." So, this indescribable infatuation is not only unexplainable, it is absolutely absurd.

I had a dream, and in it I saw a colorful, robust, blond-haired man of many years ago. He was wearing green pantaloons, a brown vest and a full, white, loose-fitting shirt. He was dancing, much like the people in the painting "The Wedding Dance" by Pieter Bruegel. When I awakened, I said with recognition, "Ferdinand!"

Frank-O was Ferdinand in a past life, I thought. I feel that he was an adored uncle, or someone else close to me, but not a mate. Perhaps that is why a closer union could never work out. It was not supposed to be that kind of relationship.

Gwenn told me that she had read that when old names entered your mind that you should write them down. They may well be names from a distant past. Now, Ferdinand had come to mind, as well as many others. She had said that these old names were probably people from a past-life experience.

I have never had any interest in history or been an avid reader, but these old names kept surfacing. Some I was sure I had not ever heard of in my life. My list was growing.

Ferdinand II, I learned, was a Holy Roman Emperor from the early seventeenth century. Obviously, if my Ferdinand were famed and he was Ferdinand I, the time period would be even earlier, I thought.

When names entered my mind, I would also note who, in this lifetime, they might now be. So far, I have identified these:

Ferdinand	Frank-O
Thaddeus	Ellen Marie
Xavier	Matt
Hortense	Sue
Maltese	Gwenn
Alabaster	
Lorenz	Chet
Horsham	Duncan
Ismael	

I generally asked Gwenn about the names as they came to me. Ismael, she told me is from the Old Testiment, about 1912. When Hortense came to mind, I told her that I felt that was Sue, but thought Hortense was a male name. Rationally, it shouldn't matter as souls may change gender from one incarnation to the next.

Why these strange names were coming to me, I didn't know. Some, I was told, were biblical names from around the 1800's to 1920's. After this brief period of recalling these names, they stopped coming to me.

Then, in reading a book based on past-life regression, a list of terms was presented as an exercise to jog past-life memories. It was a type of self-hypnosis. One is told to clear their mind; then to look at the list.

I tried this. Two words particularly provoked moving picture type memories. One had to do with war. I saw a vision of me and I was a male in army green clothing. I was approaching a hillside, with my head below the top of the hill. I was holding a rifle. I turned around where I could see my face and recognized the man as being me. I turned back around and was then shot. The shot pierced my helmet and I died.

The other vision was from the word countryside. I pictured a mountainside, sparsely covered with grass patches. In the meadow of this view was a small boy with red hair. He was about nine years old, darling, and was dressed adorably. The red hair made me think he may have been Irish. He wore green, short pants and a red-orange colored shirt or vest. I did not know who he was, but he was not me.

Sometime later, I took a trip to New Orleans with a few of my friends. I sat with Mary on the plane, and across the aisle was a red-haired man dressed in the colors of the little boy in my vision. He paid particular attention to Mary, but was outwardly friendly to both of us. I took one look at him and knew that he was the grown-up man of the little boy that I had seen in my vision.

I learned that he was from New Jersey, where Mary had been raised, and had never lived anywhere else. Trying to place that countryside vision that I had seen in New Jersey, I asked Mary about its terrain. From what I could find out, it was not at all mountainous. In all likelihood, my vision was of a land no where close to New Jersey.

I tried to make some sense out of what I had seen and to draw some conclusion as to its purpose in my life now or from somewhere in my past. I tried to identify this man with anyone that I might know now or had known. I could make no tie at all, and had to let it go. Perhaps I would receive a sign or clue at some later time.

Between the holidays of Christmas and New Years, Sue and Frank-O got together. Frank-O had gone shopping with Sue at her request, and they had stopped for lunch.

Frank-O had asked about me, and indicated he would like to stop by to see me. Obviously, it was too difficult for him to contact me on his own, but to come over with her would work. So, they stopped by and we talked.

As usual, he showed the same charmed interest he always had. Sue later told me that she thought he had wanted to invite me to a New Year's Eve party that he was having, but the invitation never came.

I woke up one morning to have these muddled thoughts enter my mind. Frank-O must have been my son in a previous life. He may also have been that darling little boy on the hillside that I adored. That is why I always tended to mother him! I also knew, instinctively, that the little boy had grown up to be the charming man that I had met on the plane. Gwenn suggested that I may have died prior to his being raised, and I was to learn that my son had gone on to do well.

This leaves a perplexing trilogy of the son who grew up to be the man on the plane, Ferdinand and Frank-O. I sense the possibility of a soul connection from different incarnations.

Chapter Twelve

The Candle's Glow
(Second Dialog)

One, evening, while sitting in my living room with Gwenn, I broke from our conversation. The sun had gone down and the daylight was leaving. Just the way the lighting was affecting the room, I could see a glow from the corner of my eye.

I said to Gwenn, "I just had a flash of a time when rooms were not lit by incandescent bulbs, but candle light. I can see the glow of the burning candle from a fixture on a wall."

"Oh, a previous life? Is it yellow?" she asked.

"Yes," I replied. " . . . a brownish yellow."

The mysterious dialog began. "What else is in that room?" she asked.

"I don't know. I just see the candle's glow on the wall. The texture of the wall is rough."

"Is there a chair in the room?"

"I don't see a chair."

"How about anything on the wall?"

I was now beginning to see more of the room. "Yes, there is a chair by the front door. And, there is something on the wall above some furniture, like a buffet."

"What is on the wall?"

"It's a gold sunburst, or a metal piece, something resembling a circle with points coming out from it."

"What are you wearing?" she asked.

"A blue, printed dress. Light material, sort of dressy. I'm waiting for my husband to come home."

"Do you have any children?"

"Yes, I have a young son."

"What is the chair like in the room? What is it made of?"

"I think it's velvet, or some smooth material."

"Look around the room. What else do you see?"

I had the strangest response to these continual questions. I wanted to say, "Look for yourself!" I then explained how strange it felt that she could not see what was in the room. She was sitting there in the same room, so why couldn't she see what I could see so clearly?

The experience was quite spontaneous, and as usual, Gwenn could pull information from me merely by asking questions. It was an unscheduled session of past-life regression. She would ask for things that I could not see until she posed the question.

From what Gwenn has read, that is similar to what happens in a hypnotic state. The person who is hypnotized sees a lot, but doesn't necessarily concentrate on the detail until asked for it.

And, so it is -- the ability to look at a past life simply from a recollection of something as a reminder -- the candle's glow. One's state of mind must be clear and relaxed for an exercise like this to produce results. I would also expect that a comfort level with the person you are with, and the acceptance and understanding of the situation to also play a large part in the ability to have this work.

I am very fortunate to have such a dear friend. She has not only encouraged me to explore this mysterious and interesting phenomenon, but she has helped me to succeed in seeing other parts of my total being.

Chapter Thirteen

Emotion

Several day trips were made with Gwenn in an effort to learn more about that haunting feeling I get when I come upon the white cinderblock buildings. Thus far, I have not been able to find such buildings in her company. They have either been the wrong type, like a barn or garage, or freshly painted and too clean, which I find to be an absolute deterrent.

My buildings must not be in a natural state of cinderblock, not be well maintained, and not be any color but a weathered white. Buildings that have vines on them may be okay if not very green; a dying vine might feel more appropriate.

Each time we ventured out with high hopes, but were disappointed when we returned home without new findings. We even took a camera to capture what we could, but were unsuccessful in finding any additional information.

Yet, while driving on my own, I would occasionally see a building that grabbed at my heartstrings. I would make a mental note to revisit it again when I had the time.

Recently, while taking an undetermined route home from a business appointment, I got lost and wandered into a strange area. I was trying to work my way back to the freeway, but had selected a street that did not have an entrance ramp to get on. I therefore drove under the freeway and then searched for a turnaround point to go back to the main road.

I selected a nearby neighborhood street in which to turn around. I noted a house which had an attached cinderblock building that looked quite ominous. Why I did not spend the time to study this place, I don't know. I always seemed to be anxious to get home, or to some other destination where I was expected to be. I would have to retrace those steps on another day and try to find this house again.

By now I had taken countless photographs of white cinderblock buildings, trying to understand the emotions they evoked and the reasons for my reactions. None of them were providing the answers that I needed.

I had visited with my daughter, Sue, recently at her condominium. I told her what difficulty I was having in defining the emotion that I felt when I came across any one of those buildings.

"It's not fear or unhappiness, per se. I'm not anxious or ready to cry. I just can't define it," I said.

Sue was pursuing a psychology degree and taking a course on emotion. I asked her, "From your emotion class, is there some kind of list of emotions somewhere that I might look at?"

"Yes, there is," she said. "I'll go out to the car and get it for you. I left my books out there."

When she returned, she handed me a paper on which there was a list of over 250 emotions. Surely I would find something I could identify with from this list.

I took the paper home and began to study it. It was divided into two categories, one of success-type emotions and the other relating to failure-type. I immediately surmised that since it was an uncomfortable emotion that it must come from the failure list.

I re-read the material I had written about these emotional experiences. I found that the only expression that I used to define what I felt was the ache in my heart. It made me think of the fear that I had been molested as a child in a previous life. What other things could provoke such an ache? I was not broken hearted. I did not feel hurt. I also considered the term forsaken.

From this list I looked up words when I questioned their meaning or wanted further definition. I began with downcast, unhappy; dejected, despondent; depressed, downhearted; disconsolate, sad, heavy, forlorn; dispirited, disheartened; doleful, woeful, dismal, mournful. Perhaps a visit back to the last place I cited would produce some new insight. All of these seemed to relate to the feeling I was trying to define, yet none felt right.

Chapter Fourteen

Closer to an Answer

I made a point to retrace my driving route to find the last cinderblock building that I had seen that might lead me closer to an answer. I was trying put myself back in an environment that would stimulate my memory whereby I could learn whatever the significant event was that had happened in such a building.

I looked at a map and followed the route I thought I had taken previously, but could not place myself in the same location again. The road dead-ended and I had already passed the vicinity of where I thought I should be. I did, however, find another such building and this time pulled off of the road to study it and try to meditate. I was not successful at finding any new information. I decided that a return to the building I had attempted to find would probably not be any more fruitful as it wasn't that good of a representation.

"I should be able to meditate and go inside such a building by myself," I said to Gwenn one day. "I can do that with other things. I can meditate and see what is happening in another person's life; why not do it with mine? Why not do it with a past life?"

"Yes, you know how to do that," she said. "Why don't you try it?"

"I guess I will when the time and circumstances are right."

I passed other intriguing buildings not far from my home, and two of them were within a mile of each other. Unfortunately, neither had a place to easily pull off of the road. I would have to travel on foot to look at either of them in detail. One was very small, close to the road, and empty. I knew it would be torn down soon as the road was going to be widened. I still did not take the time to approach the building.

One day as I passed one of these buildings, I let my mind drift. It was sort of a meditative state as I allowed my thoughts to concentrate on what was inside of the building that I saw in my mind, not the building on the street. I wanted to find answers, and I allowed my mind to go in. I could see what was in that building of my memory through my mind's eye.

I was within a room. It was very plain, almost sterile. There was no furniture in the room except for a cot alongside the left wall. I could see myself within the room looking at the cot. I had long, dark hair. I was about thirty-five years of age, which is different than the age I had thought myself to be. The younger age of around eight to ten was suggested by an inferior psychic; she thought that perhaps I had been left behind in that room to die. I knew that it was me, but the face was different than my face.

Upon the cot was a robust body curled up in a white sheet. The body was very round and must have been in a near fetal position. I could partially see the back of a male's head. I felt that it may have been my father.

I never questioned that this body was dead when my mind was perusing the bundle on the cot. I just knew it that it was. I didn't take it further to think through what might have happened to him, if he had been sick and left behind, or if he had been killed. I don't know why the room was empty other than for he and this cot. Nor do I know why I was there. I appeared still and solemn.

If this were to be a true scenario, I would need more answers. I would also need to feel the emotion that I had felt so many times before, and I did not. I presumed that it was because I saw this as an onlooker, looking at myself and the body in this room. I had to ask myself, however, "Was I getting any closer to an answer?"

Chapter Fifteen

Mutual Understanding

A couple of years had transpired and the complexity of my friendship with Frank-O continued. Our paths continued to cross because of our living in the same area and having similar interests of water and boating.

Frank-O's ex-wife had now remarried, which may explain why he had not opened up to a relationship with anyone. Perhaps he was still in love with her and awaited her possible return. He stayed pretty much to himself except for an occasional fling.

Early in the summer, Mary and I had gone to a singles' club breakfast. I was quite surprised to see Frank-O at this event. He spent some time talking with me. He explained that he had dated a friend of Marsha's, a girl with whom I had just become acquainted, but that she had gone back with her husband. I could tell that Frank-O had really liked her.

A few weeks later, my new lady friend, Marsha, and I planned to go to dinner and then to visit Frank-O and his friends at the marina nearby. After we had visited with them awhile, the group decided that we should all go to dinner. Marsha and I had already eaten, but we gladly tagged along for the company.

Marsha and I rode in the car with Frank-O and Ned. Ned drove, and Frank-O got into the back seat with me. The contact between us was powerful. He was very glad to see me, held me warmly, and the energy that passed between our held hands was full of messages. Still, we both knew that our whatever-you-want-to-call-it relationship would never be more than it was right at that moment.

Marsha had asked me previously if Frank-O and I had ever had a relationship, and I told her that we had not. I tried to explain the attachment as it was, but even I did not understand it clearly. It was one of heart-felt appreciation of one another and nothing more. I am certain that the ride in the car left questions in her mind, but she said nothing.

The next time I was to see Frank-O was on a boating trip with the club. As a club skipper, he had taken a lady and other crew on his boat, and I had traveled with Marsha on another couple's boat. Fate would have it that Frank-O docked in the next well to the one in which Marsha and I were moored.

That Friday night, I had invited my current gentleman friend to join us at the marina where we were staying in Canada. The evening found him to be obnoxious and overbearing in the company of the man whose boat I had come on. The two men competed for the attention of the crowd, and I was anxious for the night to end. I did not encourage my friend to stay the night, even though he had been invited by the boat's master. I also did not invite him to return the next evening.

The next day I learned that Frank-O's lady passenger was just that--a passenger. She had come on the trip, but they were not dating. Frank-O persisted in flirting with me throughout the day and made it known that he had been looking for me when I left the docks for lunch.

I secretly wanted to spend time with him. His gestures were inviting, but I found it difficult to manipulate the events that followed in order for that to happen. In essence, we both were probably wishing we could be together, for whatever reason, and each had an eye out for the other's whereabouts the entire weekend.

At Marsha's suggestion, she and I accompanied Frank-O on his boat for the return trip. Our captain and lady friend had become totally immersed in one another in the cabin until afternoon, and we did not wish to disturb them. Marsha seemed anxious to return home, and I was just as happy to be able to ride with Frank-O.

On the return trip, Frank-O wanted to know why I didn't ask to come on his boat. Of course, he would NEVER ask me, so that left me to always wonder if I would be welcomed.

A couple of months passed, and I had decided to take a girlfriend and my boat and spend the weekend at the marina where Frank-O and some of my other friends would be. I made an arrangement for an empty well with Frank-O, so he was aware that I would be coming.

When we arrived, he and another gal came to greet us. She was an attractive blonde, and I knew her from the club. She attached herself to him for the entire weekend. Frank-O was obviously happy that she did, but made a casual comment to me in private.

"You didn't come down here just to see me anyway," he said.

"Yes, I did!" I stated flatly. I was known to deliver succinct messages to my men friends.

Still, it was with this real understanding that we both shared that it was okay that it didn't work out.

A few weeks later I received a telephone call from Frank-O. This was quite unusual in itself. He said that he had some stock information from work and wondered if I would help him make some choices in investments. We could also go to breakfast.

I hated breakfast and knew that the stock question was just a pretense to get together to talk.

"Sure," I said, and rescheduled whatever else I had to do.

During breakfast he was compelled to explain to me how the relationship with the new girl had started, and what had transpired the day that I brought my boat to his marina. He stated that he had no intention of such an encounter that day at all. It just happened, and they now have a relationship. Admittedly, this arrangement was with some arm bending on his part, but he just wanted to explain this to me.

I told him that I loved him and was very glad for him. I meant it. Frank-O and I were never meant to have a relationship, and I appreciated his thoughtfulness and candor.

Summer was now over and so was the relationship Frank-O had with the girlfriend. He had bounced back and forth between she and the other gal, who had now definitely left her husband for good. In actuality, neither one of the girls really wanted to stay with him, and he wanted to have a real relationship.

It just so happened that I wasn't doing anything on Christmas Eve and Frank-O was having a party at his house. He invited me to come over. I was not invited as a date, and I was sure that if I had wanted to bring someone with me that it would have been fine.

The first girlfriend showed up, also by invitation, but confirmed that she was not going to be his item any longer. After she left, Frank-O's ego was bruised, and his attentions became centered on me. I knew it was a go-nowhere situation and accepted his friendship for what it was.

The following week brought another story. I learned that a second party was going to transpire at Frank-O's house on New Year's Eve. Instead of my getting an invitation, I was told that it wasn't his party and that it was being held by one of his friends. Obviously another gal of interest to him was going to be there and he didn't need me in his way.

Again time passed, and so did the girlfriends. A party took place at a mutual friend's house, and both Frank-O and I were invited. An attractive gal arrived quite late in the evening, and I liked her very much. I hadn't realized that Frank-O had taken the opportunity to ask her out.

As I was passing his house one early Friday afternoon, I saw his truck parked in the driveway and knew that he was home. I passed his house frequently, but rarely took the time to stop. This very unusual day I did stop by.

There was a small car also parked in the driveway when I arrived. I did not recognize it, but Frank-O had renters living in his house with him and I did not know their cars. The door was opened by a lovely lady. She was the girl I had met at that recent house party.

She remembered me immediately, as well as my name. At first I couldn't quite place who she was, but I knew that she was familiar. Then I realized that she was the girl that I met at the house party and had liked so well.

She and I visited and shared tea together while Frank-O went in to take his shower. She told me how favorably Frank-O talked about me.

"He loves you," she said. "He talks about you all of the time and tells me what a wonderful friend you have been to him."

I was quite enlightened by this information, as I found that I always talked to everyone else about him!

Chapter Sixteen

Some Form of Terror

Many years had passed, and I was no closer to knowing the truth of what might have happened to me in regard to that white cinderblock building many years ago. I did not know what was still causing me to gasp each time I passed one and it haunted me. I had talked to Brenda one day, a former neighbor and tarot card reader, and she asked me if I had ever figured out what those feelings were all about.

"No," I told her. "I think I need to go through a past-life regression to figure that out. I've made no progress for several years now."

"Oh, I know just the person you should talk to," she said.

"You do?" I asked with interest.

"Yes, my girlfriend, Amy. She does past-life readings. I'll give her your number and have her call you. She can't charge anything for this, but she will be glad to help you."

"That's wonderful," I said.

Gwenn had now become a registered hypnotherapist and I knew would also do a past-life reading for me. For whatever reason, the appropriate time had not presented itself, and it was never done. We seemed to manage doing our own small regression sessions without planning or preparation, but we never dealt with this issue.

A couple of months had passed, and I did not hear from Amy. When I talked to Brenda again she asked if Amy had contacted me.

"No, I haven't heard from her," I said.

"Well, I'll call her again. I'm sure you are on her list. She probably just hasn't had the time yet."

Within the next week or two, I did hear from Amy. She told me that when we met, she would place her hands on mine. If it looked as though she had information for me, I would get a reading. She explained that sometimes she finds that it is just not a good time and that the reading may have to take place at a later date. Sometimes a reading could last for five minutes and sometimes it could go on for hours.

I told her that would be fine.

"I can't charge, you know," she told me.

"Yes, Brenda told me. Why is that? Do you need to be certified or something?" I asked.

"Oh, no," she said. "My spirit guides won't let me. All I ask is that if someone else needs help and I feel you can help them that I can call on you. You will get your reading either way; it is just something that I like to do."

"Well of course, that would be fine," I said.

I took Gwenn with me and we sat across from Amy at her dining room table. She asked that I place my hands on the table and then she placed her hands on mine.

Within seconds, she told me that I had a spirit guide and that his name was Ralph. "He has red hair, a beard, and mustache," she said. "He's medium build and has blue-grey eyes." She continued, "He's jolly. He is in charge of the living of your life."

She then asked me, "Do you know Ralph?"

"No," I replied. "I don't think so."

"Well," she waited . . . The spirit guide spoke to her. "He's way out there. He lived his life and he's here to show you how to live, not to miss things. *He decided to do that.*"

Silently, she asked him how he came to be my spirit guide.

"From former incarnations, one or two as lovers, but mostly as a friend, brother or sister. You and he decided to be just friends—there was no need to be lovers."

It wasn't until much later that I considered this possibility. Ferdinand, the cute little boy on the hillside, and the red-haired man on the plane might have some connectivity with Ralph, my spirit guide.

She continued to speak the words she heard from my spirit guide. "You have a lot of passion, and you need to be carrying that passion into this life."

Amy was soft-spoken and probably in her thirties. There was nothing ominous or pretentious about her. She spoke matter-of-factly, having listened carefully to the speaker.

"There was one person in this life that you let go of, and with whom you had the potential for great passion. That was probably ten years ago, but I might not be exactly right on the timing."

She looked at me. "Was that right?"

"Yes," I had to agree. It was. That was Matt, and I had loved him dearly. Although it was clearly his choice to leave the relationship, I did let him go.

"You were afraid of losing control, according to Ralph," she said. "You easily had that fire and passion for that relationship. That is why Ralph is here, so you don't do that again. Fear. He is here to see that there is no fear of loss of control."

I had to ponder these words intensely.

"You have reached a comfort in your life, the root that is inside your soul. You are happy with your life, and you don't have to care about what others think. But you need that passion."

She listened as more messages were being delivered. She tried to put into words whatever thoughts were being fed through her.

"Let go, let the fire flow out. Enjoy life."

She paused and seemed to be finished with delivering the messages.

"Do you have any questions?" She asked me.

"Well, I came with three questions," I said.

She was open to trying to help, gesturing for me to begin.

"The first question I have is with the feelings I get whenever I see particular white cinderblock buildings," I explained. "The best emotion that I can come up with to describe what I feel is to be aghast at what I see," I said.

"Terror," she said. "The first word that comes to me is terror."

There was a pause as she listened to my spirit guide. Ralph tells her, "You were in an institution. You were a nurse. The time was about 1860. It was a mental institution."

"Was it my father that I saw?" I asked.

There was a short pause as she listened for my answer.

"No, it was not your father, but it was a man in that institution that you had a very strong affiliation with. He was a visionary. He was ahead of his time and was thought to be crazy. That's why he was in there. You were his nurse. He never left the institution; he died there."

I listened in awe. It replicated a scene in my mind that I had envisioned when I mentally took myself into that white cinderblock building—a sterile room with only a man on a cot.

"There were two men," she continued, "Thomas and Gregory. One was the patient and the other his doctor or orderly. One tortured the people in the institution. The man was dominated by a male figure. You came in afterwards and tried to sooth and comfort him. It was another power thing. You didn't speak up when you should have."

Again, the word *power* had struck my life. It had come to me previously when I asked my late grandmother for a message in regard to my purpose in this lifetime. She responded that my current life's purpose had something to do with power, but the message came when I was in a sleepy state and I could not recall it clearly.

"Gregory is coming before you leave this earth. You will know him when you see him," Amy continued. She waited as more information still came to her. "I can't tell you which man was Gregory or which man was Thomas. Trust your first instinct. Listen to the way your body reacts."

I was a little puzzled by what this all meant.

"If he is the patient, trust your instinct. You will have no love relationship with him. Don't dismiss your thought and recognition of him. Trust your instinct."

I nodded my head yes in understanding of what she had said. She asked me to go on with my next question.

"I have a question regarding a puzzling relationship in my life. It is with Frank-O. It is not a love relationship, but there is some attraction there that makes me think it is a past-life relationship."

She told me, "I feel something no good." She paused. "It's a test . . . according to Ralph," she offered. "It's a karmic lesson in this life. You chose to come together in this life for this test."

Again she said, "There is something not right about him, maybe alcohol or drugs. You are taking things into your power."

"*Power*," the word reverberated within me again.

She listened for more information from Ralph.

"He is the teacher of the lesson you are to learn, consciously or unconsciously. The lesson is – would you settle for him?" she asked me.

"No," I said. "We have no relationship. It never developed."

Now I knew, somewhere before this lifetime, that *he and I decided to be just friends—there was no need to be lovers!*

Feeling comforted by my answer she said, "Then the lesson has been learned. You will be drifting apart. The lesson is not to settle for less than what you want."

Pleased with this, she asked what else I would like to know.

"Well, my last question has to do with family spirits," I said. "I feel there are three family spirits that have to be dealt with, and I think I have defined two of the three. The first is power, and I feel that power is identified with me, as you just stated.

"The second is independence, and my cousin has identified that to be with herself. She was told by a psychic that she needed to learn independence.

"The third spirit is something I describe as sucking in. That is what came to me through my own psychic feeling, but I'm not sure what to call it. I want to tie that to the relationship with my mother. Is it to be sucked in, or withdrawn?"

Ralph, my spirit guide, said to her, "Welfare, physical and emotional. Like well-being," she explained.

Then she asked, "Is someone in the family not doing well? Or not taking care of another's well being?"

"I don't think so, but I'm not sure," I said. "Could it be a cousin from my former marriage?"

Ralph asks, "Has she spoken of a past life?"

"No," I said. "I hardly know her."

Amy continued, speaking for Ralph. "She is carrying her past lives with her."

I offered that a psychic had told her that she had died shortly before her birth into this lifetime.

Ralph says, "She is carrying it from way before that."

Amy listened and tried to decipher the messages coming to her. "She was a female leader in Athens or Greece, or maybe even Atlantis. She was definitely white-skinned. Greece – she had dark, straight hair. She wore gold.

"Maybe it was Rome and she was a Priestess," Amy offered.

She paused as she listened to glean further information. "There was a hierarchy and she carried the deaths of other people with her into other lifetimes. She was killed by the people she ruled. There was a mutiny against her."

Again she paused to get more explanation.

"She repeated this in another life. You were there, and she didn't harm you in any way. You did not have a close relationship with her in that life. You were in a lower status like a servant. You didn't convince her to stop killing people."

Another pause. "You lived to see what happened after she was killed. You stayed where you were, somewhere in the hierarchy. You didn't rise." She explained, "You were either born into the position or you weren't, and you stayed where you were in it. You were in a serving position."

Ralph offered more information. "She is here to stop carrying the people that she killed and to learn to forgive herself."

Amy listened as more information was being delivered. "She was also an Indian warrior, a male. She was the head of a slaughtering party. In that life she felt justified in the killings because she was fighting for her people. Her lesson is that you cannot justify killings. She needs to take responsibility for her actions and forgive herself."

When I met her at a family function, I learned that she had recently lost a husband; he had died in a motorcycle accident.

"Was there a lesson for her in regard to the death of her husband?" I asked.

"I'm not getting a clear answer," said Amy. She waited.

"Ralph says it was his time to go. He would have died by some other means anyway. Your death is predestined; the date and time are set and cannot be changed."

Again she listened as Ralph spoke to her.

"He is sleeping right now. He didn't learn the lesson that he was here for. He is at rest and is restoring energy. He will not be coming back in this lifetime."

She then asked Ralph if there was a karmic lesson for them but did not get an immediate answer. There was a long pause, and then Ralph began speaking.

"It was his lesson to learn and had nothing to do with her. The spirits are upset with him. She has her own lesson to learn. Compassion. She has to learn compassion."

Amy spoke. "Who had the alcohol problem?" she asked me.

"I think she did," I said. "I had heard that it was during her adolescent years."

"It is possible that she will have it again. Problems later in life could cause that."

"I'll probably be gone by then," I said.

"You will be around," said Ralph. "You live a very, very long life. You have a peaceful death, like dying in your sleep. You'll just feel 'I'm done and I'm out of here.' You will live longer than your husband, or former husband. You are single when you die."

The reading was essentially over. I had my intended questions answered, although never with the certainty that one would like to have.

"You have a group of spirit guides, obviously," Amy said.

"Obviously?" I asked. "Why obviously?"

She said, "You're right. It is not normal to have a group. It is because of the fact that you are spiritual and metaphysically inclined that you have a group to teach you. The higher you vibrate, the more help you need. The more open you are and the higher the vibration, the more helpers you attract."

"Oh," I said.

"If you can achieve living your life fully, if you can reach this, you will not have to come back."

I was astounded and filled with wonderment.

"The trust issue is a problem in living the passion. Trust yourself with who your true self is. Don't close yourself off—no, don't do that. It's more the front, or facade, than living the life the way you should."

She tried to explain. "It is as if you are hiding under a bushel basket. Remove it so that the fire can get out, and you will not have to care what others think. Trust, let your true self shine through. Let the fire out. Participate in your life. You could be right in it, not peeking out at it."

I still had another question for her. "My visions are all symbolic, but I do get them. What purpose is this to serve?" I asked.

She continued relaying messages, some of her own and some from Ralph. "Your energy should go way up when you get this feedback. That's like taking the bushel basket off and not peeking."

"Why do I get these symbolic visions?" I persisted.

Ralph says, "It's to diagnose."

"What am I supposed to do with it?" I asked.

Ralph says, "Any information you receive should be passed on. It's not a full-time job. Incorporate this into your work and make that your purpose."

Amy then directed me to close my eyes and ask about my life's purpose. "Breathe in deeply three times," she said.

I did.

"Now, one more time and tell me the first thing that comes into your mind, no matter how insignificant it may seem."

I was puzzled, for whatever I did see was quite insignificant and meaningless to me.

"What did you see?" she asked.

"I saw a blue light, perhaps a blue flame. Later, I saw a person wearing a headdress."

"Because you receive things symbolically, you may have to interpret what that means," she offered.

My thoughts were empty.

"Make sure you trust yourself. Make sure you live your life to the fullest; take all opportunities. Let go of the reins."

I tried to give her a contribution for her efforts and caring, but she absolutely would not take anything. She assured me that she was not to take payment of any kind. She had been directed by her spirit guides.

After the reading, Gwenn and I started back home, stopping for dinner and to discuss the events of the day.

"You know, the feedback on my white cinderblock building certainly corresponds with the sterile room that I had visually seen in my mind, along with the man and a cot."

"Oh, that's right," Gwenn said.

"But I may not really believe it until I've actually gone through a past-life regression, one where I really re-live the experience. No matter how painful, I may have to re-live it to believe it."

Gwenn agreed with me.

"Can you take me that deep?" I asked her.

"Yes, I can," she said.

"We'll have to do that some time."

Chapter Seventeen

Verification from Amy

Again I came upon a white cinderblock building that brought forth those horribly emotional feelings. I was now attuned to other things that I was feeling, and they were becoming more and more pronounced each time that I felt them. Now, not only did I feel the pulling at my heartstrings, but my breathing had become labored. It was short, heavy and deep. I was not gasping for air, but breathing laboriously.

It had been some time since I had seen Amy. I had tried calling her before, but did not find her at home. This was Sunday evening, and she answered the telephone.

"Hi, this is Ellen Blend."

"Oh, yes, hi."

"You remember me?" I asked.

"Yes, I do."

"Well, I'm embarrassed to call you at such a late date, but there is a question I'd like to ask."

"Sure, go ahead."

"Well, to refresh your memory, my spirit guide was Ralph and I came to you struggling to find out what perplexes me so about those white cinderblock buildings. And you told me that the white cinderblock building was an institution."

"Yes, I remember."

"Well, I was wondering if you could tell me in what country that might have been."

She hesitated a moment and then said, "The first thing that came to me was England. Does that sound right to you?"

"It could very well be. I do have English heritage, so that might fit. I might have been really excited had you told me Croatia, because I thought it might have been there."

"I'm not real good at the location of countries," she said. "But let me see." She was silent.

I knew she was concentrating, waiting to see if other information would come to her.

"No, nothing else is coming to me; I still think that it's England. Did you tell me that you knew how to do a past-life regression on yourself?"

"No, I don't think so. But I can."

"Or someone was going to do a past-life regression for you?"

"Yes, that was Gwenn, the girl who came with me to your house."

"Well, be sure that you are protected within the white circle of light when you do this."

"What do you mean?" I asked.

"You need to be in God's white light, and it usually is in a circle. Let me give you the exact wording so that you can do this. Do you have a piece of paper or something to write on?"

I moved about the kitchen to get a pen and paper and said, "Yes, I'm ready to write now."

"Oh, okay. It goes like this:

> I ask that you protect me in the white circle of light directly from God as I enter into my meditative state. Allow only truthful and beneficial information for the highest good of all to be given to me.

"You should be able to get the exact town and street name. It should all be verifiable."

"It should?"

"Sure, with the Internet today."

"Oh, I thought you meant by travel."

"Well, that too, if you want to."

"In any of your travels, have you come across a white cinderblock horse stable? That type of building also bothers me."

"Yes, as a matter of fact I have, but I don't remember exactly where I saw one."

"I have seen it a couple of times, but I cannot remember where either. I've traversed the city on every mile road and cannot find it again."

"I think it's in Washington, Michigan, on the route where I use to work, but I'm not sure where. There aren't many stables that are made of brick or stone. They belonged to the more affable and were known as gentlemen's farms."

"Well, if you see one again, would you call me?"

"Yes, I would. The things that you are remembering are from your akashic memory. It is what follows you through all lifetimes, even from the time you were just a spirit."

"Yes, I read about that in one of my books."

"If you have any other questions, even after you have that past-life regression, feel free to call."

"Thanks, I will."

Chapter Eighteen

In Search of the Stable

I had been feeling a little low for a couple of days, a condition I had not experienced for many years. "Maybe I should get a job, put my writing on hold, and go make some money," I considered. That seemed like a likely solution, but I wasn't really sure. I checked on one job that sounded palatable, but after applying heard nothing. It was probably just as well, I thought.

My horoscope had said that I would be getting some pretty strong signs from within, but thus far have had no answers. I took the day off from writing to traverse the city once again in search of that cinderblock horse stable. I knew that it was somewhere close, but I hadn't been able to find it.

I spoiled myself by getting pizza for lunch. Later, when I was getting too warm sitting in the car with the top down, I stopped at a drug store to get a pop. This was another thing that I never did. However, when I got inside the store and went to the cooler, I saw orange juice and opted for that. I'm sure it was a better choice.

My thoughts drifted to Brenda, who had read my tarot cards. She had told me that I would be meeting someone that year and that I would absolutely recognize him as someone I had known. He would be from a past life.

It was a year after having had an addition built on my home that I was reviewing some notes that I had taken from this card reading. The person who entered my life that I definitely recognized was my plumber's assistant for the new addition on my home. The first two times he appeared on the job, I questioned him extensively to find out from where I might know him.

There had been no connection that we could make, and I was not the least bit familiar to him. However, I felt strongly that I had known him well; I recognized him immediately.

Taking information from a few psychic sources, this person was to give me an indication of something important that happened in the past life with the cinderblock building. I felt that this person was the doctor's aide in a past life. He was the plumber's aide or assistant presently.

I didn't get any ill feelings from his presence or personality, so I assumed that the aide was not the person who tortured my friend in the asylum. Another piece of synchronicity was the fact that the wife of the assistant plumber had the same first name as mine.

I rode and rode all day, taking an intermission to shop for some household items. I had checked out all of the likely mile roads that I thought I had traveled before, but now wanted to check out Washington because Amy had said that she thought she saw a gentlemen's farm around 28 Mile road.

I took 26 Mile all the way out there, crossed over to 28 and made my way back. Finding no such stable, I continued to find other roads, trying 27 Mile, 25 Mile, and 24 Mile roads. I gave up the search not finding what I was looking for.

While I did not find the actual stable that I had been looking for, I found one that aroused my interest. This one was not made of cinderblock, but was white and had several glass windows. The wide stable doors were sectioned to allow the top half to stay open and the bottom closed to keep the horses inside. This was not the ideal stable that I was looking for, but it offered enough intrigue for me to stop the car and study the building.

The windows were alternately long and short, with a wide doorway in between. The windows had panes in them; the long ones had three across and four down, and the shorter ones three across and two down. The panes themselves did not mean anything to me. The shape of the long windows, however, and the white color of the building did. I squinted my eyes to see just enough to picture what I wanted from this view. It was enough to let my mind wander inside the building that was stored somewhere in my memory, not the building sitting before me.

My father was present, as he appeared to be in many of my lifetimes. We must have had a father-daughter relationship many, many times. I was a young girl, as I found myself to be in other visions with him, and then I saw a young boy. Was it me? I wondered. Was I the young boy? This time I looked at the boy and knew that he must be my brother. I have no brother in this life. I referred to my mother as Mama in this vision as I heard myself speak. My father was caring for an animal that was lying down in the stable.

It was good to feel that I had the time to stop and study the building to find what secrets it had inside for me. I have never been in a position before to do this. When working, with only a spare afternoon or day, my life was always too rushed. Now I was able to take the time, and it had paid off. I was able to learn a small piece of one of my lifetimes.

I took some pictures of this stable in case I needed to refer back to them, or was able to find a way to learn more. This building did not evoke any of those trying feelings that I found so hard to define. I obviously had a comfortable existence at this point of this lifetime. Except for the sick animal in the stable, I seemed content with my womanly chores with Mama, and my endearing feelings toward my father and brother.

I found another stable before returning home that day. It had been renovated enough to have lost its charm and ability to transmit feelings for me. It was attached to a couple of grain silos, and now had been covered over with a dark red brick.

I sat by the roadside looking upon this building. I felt grateful to have the time to devote to finding out the stories attached to the memories of my mind. This was the first time in my life that I had not felt constrained by the elements of duty and time. My spirits were now lifted and I was feeling good.

Chapter Nineteen

Venetian Festival

It was the time of an annual event among east side dwellers and boaters called the Venetian Festival. For the last few years, I had spent time during this celebration at the marina where Frank-O and other friends docked their boats.

The event contained an entire weekend filled with parties on the docks and the gathering of friends at nearby restaurants and their adjoining bars. Saturday evening was always celebrated by watching a parade of boats on the lake which were decorated with lights of various themes and followed by a gallant display of fireworks.

The crowds at this event were always so large that car entry was denied after four o'clock in the afternoon. There would be no more parking or valet space available. Latecomers had to park elsewhere and walk in.

I researched the word venetian in the dictionary and found this:

> Venetian. Of or pertaining to Venice, its culture, or its inhabitants. A native or inhabitant of Venice. Middle English, from Old French and Medieval Latin.

And, I noted:

Venetian school, a school of painting
originating in Venice in the 15th century
and climaxing in the 16th century,
notable for its mastery of strong and
deep color and perspective.

My personal perception was that Frank-O's and my prior
lifetime together must have been around the 15th or 16th
century. I related to the words of strong and deep color
as a sign in regard to the strength and depth of our
relationship.

Sometimes I attended the Venetian Festival with a date,
but this particular time I came with a girlfriend.
Frank-O's lady friend, Valerie, saw me and immediately
came over to greet me. She again began telling me how
much Frank-O loved me.

"He talks about you all of the time, and certainly more
than he talks about any other woman," she said.

Again, I was surprised to hear these spoken words from
her. Did she have any idea of the magnitude of
indescribable and intangible feelings that we shared?
They were not discernible and I could not explain them.
I wouldn't even know where to begin.

She continued. "I wouldn't say it if it weren't true. He
really does love you. I know he doesn't return your
calls, and he doesn't keep in touch, but if I could
remember what he told me, it would compliment you."

"Really!" I said. "I just consider that's the way he is, but
I know he cares about me."

"Yes, he does. He always tells me that you were always
there when he needed you, and that was during the time

he was experiencing so much pain after his divorce. He explained that when he would think of calling you, it would also remind him of all the pain he had tried to put behind him, and then he wouldn't call. He said that it was always easier to drink another beer with the guys and ignore his feelings."

I guess I had to partially understand what was contained within that message. I tried to reconstruct in my mind the conversation that must have taken place between them and that I just heard in her words. I couldn't help question what real emotion was disguised on either of their parts, or mine, for that matter.

Yet, I am still of the sound position and belief that no relationship has ever or will ever be coveted by either of us. It is this unknown, unwarranted closeness that we have and always have had that keeps me in this state of wonderment.

Before our lengthy chat concluded, I could see that she and he shared a concern about their relationship. I could relate to both of their feelings and where they were in the relationship.

Valerie was a health care professional, and her wonderful social skills, by profession, had been called upon to assist Frank-O in understanding himself, his past actions, and his emotions. She had managed to open up all channels for him, and they were all now very raw.

I was sure that he would crumble if she were to walk away. But God provides, and she was too attached to leave. At this juncture, they would painfully begin the closing process of their assignment together, or they would work out their differences and consummate a firm relationship. In either case, her gift of expressing an accurate and careful character assessment of him was exactly what he needed to help him grow.

Chapter Twenty

The Art of Pilgrimage

My British friend, Duncan, traveled to England on a regular basis. He had often asked if I would like to go with him, but I never accepted the invitation. However, I now had a definite reason to want to go. I asked if he might be going there soon.

"Yes," he said. "I will be going there next year at Easter time. Would you like to go?"

"Yes," I said, and explained my reasons and the research that I wanted to do. He seemed more than willing to accommodate me. He also requested that I partake in a canal boat trip with him that he had always wanted to take. I agreed that I would.

I was now mentally preparing for my trip to England, loosely forming in my mind the things that I would take and the places that I would visit. I actually had quite an itinerary planned from the research that I had done over the Internet; however, I knew that I couldn't possibly go to all of the locations that I had found to visit.

None of the places that I wanted to visit were tourist attractions, and they were certainly not the type of places one would ever consider visiting unless they were on a mission such as mine. Specifically, there were asylums that existed in the 1800's, tombstones of specific dimensions, street names that contained the letters c-h-e-r-t, or c-h-e-r-i-t, and land that had either as part of its name.

While doing research, I stumbled on a psychic site on the Internet that offered a free reading. One could ask a question, so I asked: *Where is the building that haunts me?* I did not receive an answer.

I followed my horoscope pretty regularly. My favorite writer always had some obscure information for me and often wrote in parables. This time he stated:

> Imagine that you've been searching for a treasure. You've scoured the world, following clues that have come to you from dreams, overheard conversations, and quirky situations. Finally, you stumble upon a large wooden chest and manage to take it home. You open it and find some of the valuables you hoped would be in it -- along with other surprises. What will you do with the contents in the years to come?

I didn't know, but I certainly couldn't imagine finding answers to the many uncertainties that I had in my life.

One evening when I was trying to relax, I watched a movie on television that took place in Ireland. I particularly liked the scenery, and the buildings were reminiscent of the buildings of my inner vision. The tombstones shown resembled more closely the size of the tombstones I wanted to find; however I found them to be more decorative than what I was looking for. I was pretty sure that I would find my exact tombstones in England.

In preparing for my trip, I wrote to many services, including the Cheltenham museum:

We have checked here in Cheltenham with our museum people and they referred us to Gloucester.

Gloucestershire Library Services have your e-mail address now and will get back to you, as there was a mental institution there dating a long time back. They will contact you directly.

Tourist Information Centre
Cheltenham

Then I corresponded with the Gloucestershire County Library.

In addition to my research of asylums, I will be researching cemeteries in England. I am particularly looking for a surname of Chert or Cherit, also around the 1800's.

Are you aware of the best way for me to search for this information via email prior to my trip in April 2001?

Other communication followed:

This is the help desk for the Gloucestershire County Library Service. We have been passed your asylums in the 1800's enquiry from the Cheltenham Tourist Information Centre.

We had two large mental asylums in the City of Gloucester, one at Coney Hill and the other on Horton Road. Both were very large institutions. To further your enquiry would you please ring our Local Studies Section of Gloucester. Unfortunately they do not have easy access to email.

Many Thanks

The list went on. Everyone was quite helpful in assisting me with my plight.

"A most peculiar itinerary," Gwenn's former husband had said to me. And yes, I agreed that it was.

I would have to select only the most important places from my exhaustive list, because even if I had the time, I would become saturated and bored. Duncan would lose patience and interest as well, and it was not my intention to take advantage of his gracious nature. We would find things to do and have fun on our journey.

Gwenn, who always mentally prepared me for things in my life, was currently reading a book on pilgrimages. Oddly enough, she was usually reading a book that directly tied in to something that I needed to know.

I had found an author of spiritual writings for her who coincidentally shared the same name as her brother. That piqued her interest; however, the spelling of the author's surname was the old spelling and not the modern-day spelling of her family name. She believed that the writer was probably related somewhere in the family line.

She bought one of his many books, and upon starting to read it said, "This may be a book you would want to read before you go. If you do, I'll let you read it before I finish it." She was always so generous with everything including her time and support.

The next time we talked she said, "From what I've read so far, you may want to take this book with you and read it on the plane. That was actually suggested in the book. It said it would be good reading while on your way to a pilgrimage."

I said that would be fine.

A few days later she reported that I would probably have questions about the things that I read, and that we should discuss them; therefore, she would read the book and we could talk about the things that she thought I should know prior to going. I was happy with this as well. She would finely tune and select the things that she felt were pertinent to me and give me her verbal comments.

This morning she reported that my quest was not just a quest. I was going on a pilgrimage. A pilgrimage would discover information and give me challenges along the way. It would be my soul's journey, and not just a trip to look for the things that I knew I wanted to find. In fact, I may not find any of the things that I really went there for, but that I should let my soul take me to the places it needed to go, and let it find what it needed to see. I could look at buildings and tombstones, but I should reflect upon each to let them give me information. That would meet the requirements of a real pilgrimage.

I said that I wasn't really sure what I was looking for at all. I just had clues of information that were to lead me to whatever it was that I needed to learn. And, I wasn't sure that I would be able to satisfy my own needs for these things at all. I did understand, however, that I was being driven to look for whatever it was that I needed to know. What I didn't realize was that it was my soul that was directing me all along; not my psyche, not my intuition, and not my own intelligence.

She also advised that I should sit down and think about these things before I go. I should reflect upon any recurring dream that I had ever had, or any dream of significance for that matter. I should also think about the things that I played with as a child, and where my young imagination had taken me. I should revisit those paths in my mind, and open up those channels again-- those imaginative channels that you have as a child.

She suggested that when I did come upon a tombstone that resembled the characteristics of the ones in my search, that I should reflect upon whatever information it could give me. I should take the time to meditate, even if the name of the tombstone meant nothing to me. This would allow my soul to find the path to take me where it was that I needed to go.

I told her that I would do that. I would allow myself this opportunity. I would seek out what it was that my soul wanted me to do. Surely, I now understood that it was my soul that was directing me.

Chapter Twenty-One

The Trip to England

This was probably the easiest trip that I had ever packed for. Normally I would not be able to decide what to take and spend the last day repacking because I had changed my mind about what I was going to need. Perhaps because I was not working at this time, I was allowed the opportunity to more fully coordinate the clothing that was interchangeable and workable for what I expected to need.

Our flight was not until 9:30 p.m., and Duncan had said that he would be over around 6:30 in the evening. I had agreed to drive to the airport; so in the afternoon, when I was completely ready, I took the car up to the gas station to fill up.

On my way, I saw a bird dive toward a car in front of me; however, the force of the air from the moving car blew it out of danger. The bird again swooped around and dove into oncoming traffic as if it were on a suicide mission. I wondered what could have happened in that little bird's life that it wanted it to end.

The trip began, and we were now on the plane. It was Saturday, April 7, and we were to arrive in London on Sunday, April 8. I had taken my shoes off as my feet had become swollen, and I wanted to be comfortable in order to sleep on the plane. Duncan and I had each had a small bottle of wine, fitting for a relaxing evening. I had a small amount left in my glass. An attendant reached over to pick up the empty bottle, knocking red wine into my shoe. I was not about to let that little incident upset my pleasant mood.

A thunderstorm was in our flight path, and the pilot announced that we would be flying north of the storm. I watched lightning in the sky closer than I had ever seen it before. It was beautiful as it lit up the sky over and over again.

I slept for a few hours and was awakened at 3:00 a.m. Daylight had arrived, and I could see the sun's gorgeous pink glow over the vast ocean. It was a beautiful sight, but clouds soon covered the air and I could no longer see the water.

Our plane arrived safely on the ground at Heathrow Airport. We picked up our luggage and found our way to the rental car agency to begin our journey. Already I was seeing the difference in signage from my country. A sign read "baggage reclaim" instead of "baggage claim," and on the road, "no hard shoulder" rather than "soft shoulder."

Shortly after leaving Heathrow Airport, I saw a sign that read "Six Miles to Chertsey." Chertsey was a city that I planned to visit since it contained the letters c-h-e-r-t. We would take the Great Chertsey Road.

Duncan asked if I wanted to go there now, but my need for something to eat and a restroom seemed more important. I was rather tired, and traipsing through cemeteries and perhaps a visit to the Chertsey Library and museum did not seem appealing so early in my journey. Duncan said that we would have another opportunity on our way home from Wales. I wasn't sure that would be the route, but felt comfortable that we would get there.

The roadways were traveled by fast little cars that reminded me of matchbox car races. I had heard about roundabouts from Duncan, but now I could see them first hand. When approaching an intersection, I found a circular drive with many highway signs and roads branching off from the circle.

Duncan explained that sometimes you had to circle a couple of times if you weren't in the right lane to exit where you wanted, or weren't sure which road you needed. Fortunately, he had the experience of driving on the left-hand side of the road and did not ask me to drive. Even he, having driven these roads before, was honked at a few times until he got the hang of it.

We got something to eat at a quaint English Pub which had been converted into a restaurant as well. I was also beginning to see tile and slate roofs, not common to Michigan.

The food was great, and Duncan was able to enjoy his first pint of English beer. He claimed that England does not use the chemicals in their alcoholic beverages that we use in the United States, which accounts for a far better taste. He also said that because of this, I wouldn't ever get a hangover in England.

We eventually arrived at Duncan's brother's house, and were welcomed by Arthur, his wife, and three darling children. The oldest was a nice young lady of twelve, and the next was the most animated, friendly child I had ever met. She was extraordinary to say the least. For four years old, she was quite adult and logical. Duncan told me that Arthur was just like her as a child. The baby, a two-year old boy, was quite shy and was put to bed shortly after we arrived.

Arthur looked so much like Duncan that I was astonished. They were half brothers, but the similarity was remarkable. They both had dark hair and very good looking faces. Arthur was charming, a great conversationalist, and a wonderful family man. It was clear that the children all loved him; they climbed all over his lap trying to be near him. His wife, Marie, was more subdued. Duncan had mentioned that she was always pleasant, but never outwardly welcoming due to her quiet nature.

Duncan's only request of this travel was to take a boat trip along one of the canals in England. He had asked me to search the Internet for canal boat companies, which I did. To my surprise, all boats were "narrow boats" and had to be rented a minimum of four days and nights. There would be no captain; we would be taking the boat out by ourselves. Since I was a boater, Duncan thought it would be perfect for us to do this. He had wanted to take a boat trip like this for many years, but he needed a boater with whom to share the experience. That was me.

A boater I was, but taking a fifty-foot boat by ourselves, when I didn't think Duncan would be much help, did not seem appealing. It sounded like a lot of work. When I learned that each of the canals contained a certain number of locks that we would have to go through, I became really worried.

Duncan said, "Oh, they're easy. I watched someone open and close the locks. It's not hard." That gave me a little confidence.

It was the only real request Duncan had, and he was kind enough to accommodate my peculiar agenda—chert rocks, cemeteries, insane asylums and old cinderblock buildings. Besides, since he could drive there, he could take me to the obscure places that I needed to go. None of the tourist forms of transportation would go where I wanted, and I was most appreciative of Duncan's generosity. I agreed to the boat trip. I was dreading it, but I agreed.

As it turned out, Duncan surprised me and ended up to be a very good boater. Between us, we handled the boat, swinging bridges, and locks just fine. I'm sure that Duncan would like to take another such trip some time on another canal. After all, there are more than 3,000 miles of waterways in England.

Our boat trip was to begin in the city of Bradford Upon Avon and our destination was Bath. Prior to picking up the boat by 5:00 p.m., we toured a town called Newbury. Duncan and I each had a friend who had some association with Newbury, and he wanted me to see the town. It was also a nice place for us to have lunch on the water.

It was a very clean and upper-class town, and we watched other boaters maneuver through the locks as we ate. We met some darling children who were enjoying their first day off of school for Easter break. Each child was very well dressed. They called us Americans, and entertained us with their chatter.

When we returned to our rental car, a ticket had been slapped onto the windshield. "What for?" I wondered.

Duncan removed the ticket to find that it was a "pay and display" lot. That meant to pay for the parking and display the ticket in the front window, and we had failed to do that. The ticket amount was 50 lbs., which would have equated to $75.00. Since it was before 5:00 p.m., Duncan insisted that we go directly to the county building and that I tell them that I had parked the car.

"They're a lot easier on women," he said.

So I tooked the ticket and explained that I had parked the car not realizing that it was a pay lot. My American accent was obvious, and they asked me to sign a paper and eliminated the fine entirely. It was probably better that Duncan didn't speak, as his British accent would surely have been noted. I could see that they wouldn't have been as lenient with him.

Duncan and I were briefed by the boat marina personnel on what to expect, what was on the boat, where the propane gas for heat was, about the water controls, etc. We were ready to be on our way. It would be dark within an hour, so we wouldn't travel much this first day. One of the workers had told us that there would be a grocery store not far from the marina. It would be a good place to shop and stop for the night. We could moor anywhere along the canal that we liked.

We found the first stop, walked to the store, and bought things like milk, juice, coffee, lunch meat, cheese, crackers and wine. We dined at an elegant Chinese restaurant where the food was unique and exquisitely prepared. We tired of the background music before leaving, as the same CD had repeated itself four to five times. About the third time, Duncan asked about the music, hoping to alert them that it had been playing for some time. However, they just explained what the music was all about, and it continued to grind on him throughout our meal.

When we returned to the boat in the dark, we found that one of our mooring lines had broken loose, stake and all. The boat had drifted sideways across the canal. Since the boats were to be still by sundown, it was unlikely that anyone had tried to pass. It was now after 11:00 p.m., the wind had picked up, and we were unable to pull the drifted end of the boat back into shore without a line.

One end of our boat had drifted to rest on a moored boat on the opposite side of the canal. I tried to push our boat off of the moored boat, but the wind quickly pushed us back. We finally agreed that there was no other choice but to start the engine.

The engine roared in the silence of the night. We knew that we were disturbing other boaters as well as those in apartments or housing alongside the canal. Each time Duncan tried to put the boat in gear, however, it would lock up and the engine would stall. We were getting nowhere. Duncan let the engine run to see if that might stop it from stalling, but someone yelled out, "Turn that engine off!"

Duncan obliged as quickly as he could, and a "Thank you!" rang out from the hillside. We chuckled, but I'm sure it was disconcerting to Duncan to say the least. We still had to re-secure the boat. Since we couldn't move the boat, we let it drift to the opposite side of the canal and tied up to the boat we had accidentally moored against, not asking for permission. It appeared that the occupants had retired for the evening, and we hoped that they wouldn't mind and would notice us in the morning before trying to leave!

Duncan then tied the other end of the boat to an overhanging tree branch, as we could not get any closer to the shoreline where we were. I had my doubts as to the strength of that little branch, but how far could we go on a narrow canal anyway? We drank a bottle of wine and then went to sleep for the night.

Chapter Twenty-Two

The Next Morning

Duncan and I had our morning coffee, and he watched for the couple in the next boat to arise. When the man came out on the back deck, Duncan explained what had happened. He was assured that it was no problem as they hadn't planned on leaving until afternoon.

Duncan then walked into town and telephoned the boat company to come and look at the boat. By now we realized that we had picked something up in the canal and it was wrapped around the prop.

We had picked up a bicycle tire in the canal. It was not just the rubber tire, however; it was the rim, spokes and all, tightly wound around the prop. The boat company removed it piece by piece, and we were on our way by noon. I was hoping that each day would not bring such an event.

At this point I had not driven the boat at all, and frankly I was scared to death. The young man from the boat company offered to help us through the first set of locks since they were just ahead. He assured me that there would be a long stretch ahead of us and plenty of time to get accustomed to the boat before reaching the next lock. I was grateful.

When we reached the first lock, the assistant said that one should remain on the boat, and he would instruct the other on how to open the lock. Since I was still afraid of the boat and going through the lock, I offered to be shown how to open it.

The lock was manual, and a tool was on the boat which was to be used to open the lock. He demonstrated how to use the tool to lift the lock, which allowed the water to begin flowing underneath. When enough pressure had been released, the lock gate would then swing open more easily. Then it was time to cross over the bridge and do the same thing on the other side—by myself.

I found that I didn't have the physical strength to close the lock gate myself after the boat had gone through, and that was part of the job. Now I was really in a fix, I thought. Someone came to assist me.

We were on our way again, and the scenery along the canal was much more interesting than I had ever imagined. Our next encounter was a swinging bridge; and, as we approached, someone on land kindly opened the bridge and waved us through.

As we traveled along, I then got brave enough to take the tiller in hand and managed to learn how to control the speed of the boat. Needless to say, travel was slow as there was to be no wake in the canal at any time.

We passed many farm lands, tremendously old buildings, and suddenly, I remembered. I remembered a dream, a childhood dream, of going up and down streams of water in a boat. I remembered a childhood fear of my mother going away in a boat, and being afraid that she would not return. I had been left with my grandmother, but I was frightened that I would not see my mother again. Then I remembered other times of being a little older and enjoying the excitement of the boat ride and the beauty of the winding canals and overhanging tree branches. It was then that I knew that I had been on the canals of England before, and that it hadn't really been a dream at all. I had experienced childhood memories from another lifetime. I was astounded at that realization.

Duncan and I continued on our way, and I explained of the recollection of what I had thought to be a childhood dream. I went over and over what had seemed like a dream and tried to determine what the elements of the dream were about.

Now another childhood dream or memory came to mind. It took place at the top of a very wet and steep hill. I thought of this hill as a wet grassy knoll. I remember being afraid to go down that hill, but that I must do it. Other family members were sliding down, too, but I must go down alone. It was the only way to get to the meadow below. It was a long way down, and I was afraid. My uncle convinced me that the deep crevices formed by the water's runoff would keep me on course and that I must go next.

That evening Duncan and I walked into town after having docked for the night. We found a pub and had dinner and drinks. Later we played darts, which he had brought along, and watched two teams of gentlemen play skittle, a type of bowling.

I had too much coffee during the evening and was unable to sleep most of the night. I used that time to go over the two dreams I had remembered. Over and over them I went, trying to remember the details. A third dream now came to mind. It was one that I could never sort out as a child. It was so real that I tried to place it in this lifetime, but could never be sure that it had really happened.

In this lifetime, my cousin and I had played in a field where there were new houses going to be built. The basements had been dug, and we played on the mounds of dirt. In my dream, if it was a dream, I remembered going through very long tunnels, but I couldn't fathom going through tunnels of dirt from the mounds that I remembered.

My uncle had been there peering through the end of the tunnel to see me. It was so real, but I couldn't remember the tunnels actually being on that lot where they were building the houses. I now thought that perhaps this memory was actually of some caverns or tunnels in a mountainside, but I wasn't sure. Why else did this memory come to me at this time if it did not pertain to England?

"Yes, Diane," the words were heard in my head, as conversation was directed to either my mother or myself. I could sense us both in the room, but I didn't know who was talking or to whom the words were spoken. I supposed that my mother's name in that lifetime was Diane and that the words were said to her.

"That's right, George," I later heard my mother say. It was my mother, but not the voice I knew to be hers in my current life. It was a previous life to be sure, and George may have been my father, but I could not see him in the vision before me.

My thoughts drifted as I still lay awake that night. I watched as I was being lowered into a cylindrical tank. I was a man, I was wearing a helmet, and dark smoke was coming out of the tank. I guessed my age to be about thirty to thirty-five. The tank was made of rectangular pieces of metal. Some form of welds or fasteners had secured the pieces. What lifetime and period was this, I wondered. Where did this take place?

The next morning Duncan and I completed our trip to Bath, a very old Roman town. It was a magnificent sight to see beginning with the approach of the city. We visited a Roman Bath that still exists today, and later had dinner in one of the local pubs not too far from where we had moored our boat. An Irish gentleman introduced himself, and then us to some of his friends. Later, he took us on a tour of pubs in the immediate area and entertained us for the evening.

In the morning we would head back on our two-day return trip to Bradford. Next we would drive to Wales to stay in a Castle.

Chapter Twenty-Three

A Magical Land

We were now on our way to Ruthin Castle. Although we were headed toward northern Wales, we drove through England until we were quite north, and then went west into Wales.

I took in the scenery along the way, and the setting felt very magical to me. I couldn't reason why, as I had certainly seen beautiful landscapes of gentle mountains, green hillsides, and bodies of water before; but, it just felt magical. I could feel the history of many years' prior living and the legends of people on that very land.

On our drive to Ruthin, I learned that there was a grassy limestone area of England. I thought about the wet grassy knoll of my recent memory. We passed two very wet areas of grass, but not on an incline as I had remembered. I was sure that it existed, however, as England's grass is very green and it rains nearly every day.

I picked up a brochure on slate caverns. Duncan claimed that they were not too far from Ruthin Castle where we would be staying. Perhaps visiting them might awaken thoughts from my memory of a long, dirt tunnel. We would be there for two nights, so we would have time to visit them. Duncan was so helpful in accommodating anything that I felt would help me on my quest.

We arrived at Ruthin Castle. We were just in time for afternoon tea and pastries, which was immediately followed by a happy hour in the Castle lounge. The

Castle was lovely, and that evening we dined with an exquisite meal of our choice from the menu.

On Saturday we drove further north in Wales to Snowden, and took a train to the top of the mountain. We passed many cobblestone walls near Llechwedd on our way to Snowden. Duncan had made this trip before, but he thought that I would enjoy it. What I really enjoyed was the fact that the train departed from a coal-mining area, as my father had worked in the coal mines in Pennsylvania when he was a young boy.

Later that day, we drove to the slate mines and caverns. We took a deep mine tour, which we enjoyed, but I did not find anything reminiscent of my childhood dream or memory of tunneling through dirt.

We returned to Ruthin Castle in time for the Medieval Banquet. We were escorted to the head table, along with a couple who was celebrating the young man's birthday. They were appropriately dressed in costume for the occasion.

Our dinners were consumed with only a sharp knife, and we dunked delicious bread in a tasty soup. When we ran out of bread, we drank the soup from our bowls. Dessert was a light lemon-type pudding; and we drank red wine and mead, which was made from fermented honey and water.

Chapter Twenty-Four

Psychiatric Hospitals of the 1800's

It was Easter Sunday, and we were on our way to Stratford Upon Avon, the Shakepearean town. Because it was a holiday, no plays were performed that day. We enjoyed walking through the town and taking in the scenery on the River Avon. We had a drink at The Old Thatch pub which had been named for its thatched roof.

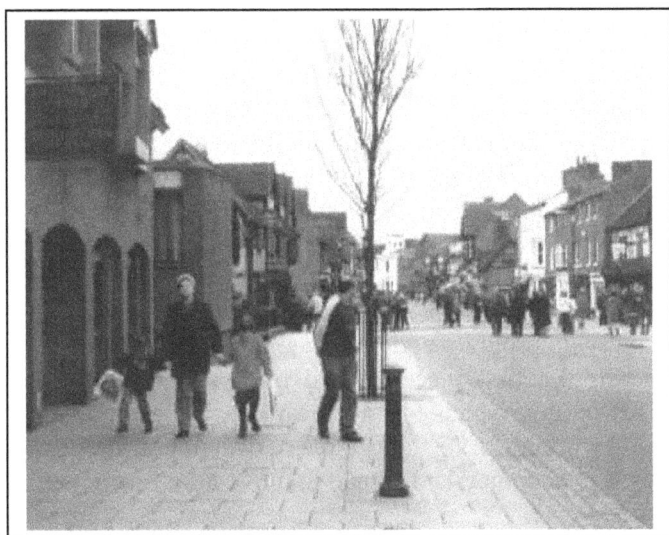

I felt the presence of my uncle from this life strongly in my past. I even wondered if perhaps he was George. I ended up settling on George being my father, but I certainly could not be sure.

As Duncan and I sat in the Old Thatch, he noticed a man unloading band equipment from his vehicle and taking it into the White Swan Hotel. We went there later to be entertained by a jazz band. They also played a few selections of Motown music.

We stayed the night at a bed and breakfast called Nardo's. Breakfast was served in a central dining area. It was a typical English breakfast of eggs up, toast, marmalade, ham, sausage, baked beans and tomato (pronounced toe-maa-toe). That proved to be entirely too much food for me, so I settled for one egg and toast. Duncan, however, many times enjoyed this entire English presentation.

Easter Monday we were to begin the search for the lunatic asylums of the 1800's. I had selected only two from the many I had researched on the Internet. It was difficult to choose, but one was in Nottingham and the other in Leicester.

On our way, near Coventry, Duncan saw a sign for Coombe Abbey. At the age of nineteen, he had been on an apprenticeship program and had lived there for a short time. It was the first place he had lived away from home. This program entailed three years of college and one year of working. Not long after he was there, the building was condemned and he had to move into town.

The building had now been restored, and its interior was the most beautiful building I had seen in England. It was elegant. I believe the figure quoted to restore it was equivalent to four and a half million dollars. It has now been converted into a hotel, and to stay in the best room would cost about five hundred American dollars per night.

A new entrance adorned the lobby, and confessionals had been brought in to be used as telephone booths. Duncan recognized the telephones to be like the ones that he built when working for the company that sponsored his apprenticeship.

I related to having been in the confessionals as a young girl. I would judge my age to be about seven, but I had never been in one in my current lifetime. I reasoned that I must have belonged to the Church of England nearly a hundred years ago.

In conversation with Duncan, he mentioned that the English rarely say "excuse me" when accidentally bumping against you in a crowd. They would say, "sorry." I noted that I said sorry, too.

"I've noticed other things you say, too, that are very English," commented Duncan.

Was that part of my soul that followed me into this life? Was that my akashic memory?

Then I asked, "Do English people say hello or hi when greeting someone?"

"Always hello; never hi," said Duncan.

"I always say hello, too. Whenever anyone greets me with a hi, I always respond with hello. I noticed that myself," I commented.

Very interesting, I thought. I also wondered why I insisted on spelling the color gray g-r-e-y. I knew that it was listed as a variation in the dictionary, but Duncan confirmed that g-r-e-y was the English spelling.

We had now arrived at Mapperly Hospital in Nottingham, a building so huge that it went on for the equivalent of three city blocks. It was a red brick building, which I knew it would be from the picture and description I had received from my research.

The building was no longer a psychiatric hospital; it was part of the Nottingham University. It now had a Division of Psychiatry and a School of Nursing.

I had corresponded with a gentleman at the university hospital prior to my traveling there. He provided me with a slim booklet about the history of Mapperly Hospital.

The booklet stated that The Lunacy Act of 1890 granted admittance of private paying patients. The hospital could also accept voluntary patients who felt that they could no longer provide for themselves on the streets. In addition, the Mental Treatment Act of 1930 stopped the isolation of mental patients. I also learned some interesting historical data such as an outbreak of small pox in the city between 1914 and 1918, and that electricity was installed there in 1924.

Since my search was starting with minimal information, I was curious as to the grounds and equally interested in the walls of the inside of this vast building. Because of the holiday, no one was there to allow entrance. I peered in the windows, but could only see smooth plaster walls; they were not made of block.

I noted the abbey, which I had read was above the dining hall. I did not get any feelings in regard to the building. I could somewhat relate to the grounds, but with no real relevance.

We circled this huge mass of a building. I was convinced that there was nothing there for me until I saw a walking path with a steep decline and a high stone wall on one side.

I felt that I had walked up and down that path with friends as a young girl on my way to and from school. I remember letting my hand reach out and touch that stone wall as I walked up the hill. I even remember my cousin from this life being among the children.

As I look at the photograph now, I can see a white house at the base of the walking path. I wonder if it is made of block. Also, the high stone wall is now heavily covered with vines, but it wasn't when I was a child.

I felt that in later years I may have gone to nursing school there, and had walked down that path to go home each evening.

We got back into the car, and as we drove along, I saw many buildings made of red brick. Red soil was quite prevalent in this area. I didn't particularly like the looks of the red buildings; I longed for the stone that I had seen in other parts of England. The red brick was too similar to what is used in the United States, and I was enjoying the stones of English charm.

As my mind took a momentary sabbatical, I could see the process of making bricks. I saw the red soil made into a liquid form, the transferring of it from an open sheath, or what appeared to be half of a vat, and it being poured into a trough.

I also saw a man's cart with the name Smede and Son on the side and knew that it belonged to my father. He was in the brick-making business. Perhaps he even used the canals to transport the bricks.

My thoughts rested on the *and son,* and I thought, "Oh, yes, I had a brother. Hank."

Now I had names. Perhaps my father's name was George Smede, my mother's was Diane Smede, and my brother's was Hank Smede. These would certainly be traceable somehow.

I recalled a previous vision that I had seen some time ago of my father feeding chickens in the yard and of my brother helping him. I had come outside to see them and then returned inside to assist my mother in the kitchen.

I had much research to do, and upon returning home I learned that the transporting of bricks by canal peaked in the 1800's.

The canal-side brickworks company of Orlando Brothers was located in Blackburn around 1879. Another company was the Livesey Fire Clay Works which began around 1835, before also coming under Orlando Brothers, and operated until its closure in 1894.

A map showed that it was located between Brothers Street and the Green Lane bridge, and that it crossed over the canal. It was being supplied by an elevated tramway with material from a fireclay pit a few hundred yards to the south.

Other companies were the Accrington Brick & Tile Works, 1887; Ganister Fire Clay Works, 1894; and Shaw Glazed Brick Co., 1897.

The following day Duncan and I began our journey to Leicester. Our next quest was to find the Tower Hospital. This city was older and less attractive than other cities we had been in. I felt a little uncomfortable in the surroundings.

The hospital was close to the heart of the city, but the streets were small, parking was tight, and the directions were deplorable. It was difficult to get around the narrow streets.

Duncan was quite industrious in finding police stations, libraries, real estate offices and shopping malls with bookstores to find maps and directions to these obscure places on my list. His patience and tolerance were quite commendable.

There were times I felt sorry that I had dragged him into such abhorable excursions. No one should have had to work so hard for something that was of no consequence to him. He never complained, and was most willing to accommodate my every whim.

When we arrived at the Tower Hospital, there were relatively few staff members on site. The exterior of the building had been transformed from a stucco appearance to a bricked state that I would no longer recognize.

We entered the lobby, and I was able to see the interior walls of the hallways and adjoining office area. They were not made of block, and the exterior was now a red brick, just as Mapperly Hospital had been.

Someone had kindly sent me pictures of what the hospital and grounds had looked like prior to its having been rebuilt. One picture showed the hospital to be white with an adjacent ground called Abbey Park. This old picture was quite omnipotent and a place I wanted to see, but existed no longer. The transformation had made the area quite unfamiliar to me.

This hospital was of enormous size and was called The George Hine House. It was now a medical research facility. Duncan encouraged me to ask any questions that I might have, and to see if someone could give us a tour. I approached one of the ladies in the front office from the lobby window.

The lady was very kind and made a couple of calls, but she could find no one on staff to give us a tour. She provided me with a name and telephone number and asked that I call for an appointment. Someone would surely be able to give us a tour.

I thanked her kindly, but knew that there was nothing further that I needed to see there. If I had ever worked in this hospital, I could only relate to it in its original form of the 1800's.

That evening we went to dinner at an Indian restaurant. Duncan always talked to the staff or anyone seated near us. In his company I was able to experience a real cultural education. In Chinese restaurants I met English people from Hong Kong, and in this restaurant English people who had come from India. I had no idea that there was an English sector in any of these countries. Duncan also made a point to have each person that had been raised in England speak to me so that I could hear the difference in dialogs from the various cities.

After dinner, we went to a show at a movie theater near our hotel. We saw the Wedding Planner with Jennifer Lopez. It was very entertaining and we both enjoyed it.

I did not feel an attachment to anything in this town and felt that I had never lived there. I may have related to the old Tower Hospital in its original form, but its transformation left no identity for me.

Chapter Twenty-Five

My Land and Tombstones

Our next stop was London, where we took in a few sights using the London Underground. We saw the London Tower, Tower Bridge, and Buckingham Palace.

We stayed at a very nice downtown hotel called the Selfridges, with attached shopping, and made a reservation for a play with the hotel concierge for that evening. The hotel was quite reasonable for a heart-of-the-city room, but the parking for one night amounted to fifty dollars in American money!

We saw an entertaining and well-performed musical at the Prince of Wales Theatre in London. It was called "The Witches of Eastwick," and suited the theme of my travels.

I had taken ill with some kind of virus, I presumed, and returned to the hotel with the worst shivers and shakes I had ever remembered having. They were accompanied by a sore throat and swollen glands, and by morning I could hardly swallow. I felt sure that I was going to need a doctor; the few antibiotics I had with me were not enough to get me feeling well again. While Duncan still slept, I ordered room service of juice and coffee.

When Duncan awoke, I told him how poorly I felt. He explained that I would lose an entire day if I needed to go to the doctor, because they were only available for emergencies in hospitals. He implied that I could just forget about being sick.

The coffee and juice made me feel more human, and I sparingly took part of another antibiotic that I had with me. I felt some better. From then on, I quartered the pills I had left and took a portion each time the chills returned. Somehow, miraculously, and with a talk to God, I persuaded him to let me feel better until I got home.

God listened and I got better. The illness returned when I got home, and I took the rest of the antibiotics that I had there. I soon recovered.

As we drove along, my eyes peered wide at each thing that I saw that might be a link to information that I needed. I made several notes for possible future research. We passed a Courage building, which was a brewery of an English beer, and I noted a large silver tank on land nearby. We were somewhere between Newbury and Reading.

I noted Tilehurst, a company I thought might make the stone I was looking for, and a sign noting Bath Hospital. We were still in the same vicinity. Then I wrote Thermocrete, where I also noted River Cherwell and the city Chipping Norton.

We now were approaching the Cotswolds area which was between Oxford and Gloucester. We stopped at the first cemetery I was to walk through and I found several tombstones of various styles. To my surprise, the years were in the 1800's, and many 1880's.

I had carried a tape measure conveniently in my handbag for just this occasion. I found exactly the tombstones that I had been looking for. They were made of chert, both a grey-white color and the combination of other colors of red, green and brown.

I began to write down the years of death and the measurements of similar stones. The city was Banbury.

1888	23" wide x 3" deep
1871	27" wide x 3" deep
1903	27" wide x 3-1/2" deep
19??	29" wide x 3" deep

I had missed writing the year down of the last stone noted. Interestingly, each of the headstones that were exactly what I was looking for were all in the 1880's and measured exactly 27" wide by 3" deep.

145

Quite near the cemetery was the Southam Road Evalangical Church, which was near a Volkswagen dealership.

We got back into the car again and continued our journey. With pen and paper handy, I again made note of Wykham Mill. I'm not sure what significance this was to have other than to identify the location as to where I was.

A while later, a sign read Lansdown Close, and I knew that there was going to be a piece of significant information come to me soon due to the synchronicity in the message. I was raised on a street called Lansdowne in Detroit, Michigan. Lansdowne was my homeland, and I knew that my homeland of many years prior was now very close.

There it was, a very green and steep hillside. It not only was wet, as I had remembered it as a small child in that previous life, but it had the distinct, evenly spaced vertical grooves in the land from the run off of water going down the hill. The crevices were a natural formation, and I remembered my uncle convincing me that I would be all right going down that hillside. He explained that the ridges would keep me in the path that I would need to follow on my way down.

Banbury was just below Coventry and right above Oxford, about the same distance from each city. I now felt strongly that this was exactly where I had lived in the past. Perhaps one of the waterways that I remembered was actually the River Cherwell.

One type of tree in particular caught my attention throughout the country parts of England. I was sure that I had lived with one of these trees near my home. It gave me a warm-hearted feeling. It was a very woody tree with heavy branches and snaking limbs. Most of the trees were still barren, so the thick, woody branches of these particular trees were all exposed. I asked Duncan if he knew what kind of tree it was.

"Probably Conker, Ash or Elm," he said. He wasn't sure. I didn't think it was a tree that we had in the United States, so I thought perhaps it was what he called Conker. I would look it up from home later. The trees in their barren state told me that I had lived near one before. I wondered what they looked like with leaves on them.

When I later questioned Duncan about the Conker tree, he told me that it was the same as a Horse Chestnut tree. That is a tree that is also in the United States, but not very prevalent. Later research confirmed that the tree name that I had been looking for was actually Oak.

We continued to ride along beautiful winding and narrow roads, and I was busily noting signage. I was amused with one with such literal meaning. It read, "Oncoming Traffic in Middle of Road."

One more small revelation was to come to me now. I saw my mother coming out of our house. It had a bay window, quite common in England, and she was walking through a very narrow doorway. The spirit world has a way of giving you only the information that you need. I did not see the whole exterior of the house, only the window and door. The door was significant because it was so narrow.

Doors in the United States usually have widths of 2-1/2 feet for interior and 3 feet for exterior. The door that I saw was an exterior door and was probably no more than 20 inches in width. That was significantly more narrow than normal and would also be the clue to exactly the type of home or location in which I had lived. I wondered if it still existed. I suspected that it did.

I now had much to think about, having had three childhood dreams come to me that I hadn't thought about in more than fifty years. Only they weren't dreams at all; they were childhood memories from another lifetime.

I also had names, my father's business of making bricks, and some brief vision of me as a male being lowered into a huge tank. I had no idea that I would have so many revelations come to me from taking this trip. I had resolved myself to the fact that I might return with nothing but fond memories, but that is not what happened at all.

Gwenn remarked upon my return and news, "So you touched the sacred ground. I knew that as soon as your feet touched the vintage soil that you would find what you were looking for. That is the real art of a pilgrimage."

Chapter Twenty-Six

The Cotswolds

On Thursday, April 20, 2001, we were now in the Cotswolds. It was a beautiful sunny morning in this quaint village. Duncan and I took pictures as we walked through the town, and I peered in the windows of upscale shops.

We had stayed at the Royalist Hotel, built in 947 A.D. It was on Digbeth Street in Stow-on-the-Wold. It was hard to imagine how these very old buildings and cities were kept up so well.

We met a delightful couple in the restaurant that evening and saw them again at breakfast. They had two well-behaved dogs with them that were allowed to sit by their feet at the table.

The couple had just bought a second home in Stow-on-the-Wold, and were going to close on the property that day. They were partners with someone else in a small book binding and book restorer business, which would free them up to use their home on the water on alternate weeks. I was very pleased for them.

We exchanged information so that we could correspond later, and upon my giving the gentleman my business card he responded, "Smashing!"

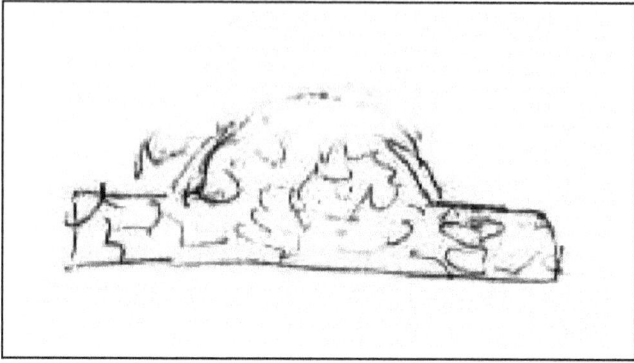

I had trouble sleeping at night, and in the morning I told Duncan of my latest revelation of the dark hours of the evening before. I actually had two pieces of information come to me, and I grabbed a pad of paper and a pencil from the nightstand. I couldn't get to the paper fast enough, and although I am sure the first information was about my mother, the message was lost in its entirety.

What I did capture was the information that follows. This is what I wrote:

> 1925. Boy of 12. Lived at a castle. Dingy castle with gold Roman letters around an arched opening. I could see deep down into a center hole that felt like a dungeon. My name was Charles.

I could see a large archway with gold Roman letters across the top, but I couldn't read them. I roughly sketched the arch as best as I could on another sheet of paper. I tried to draw what I saw in my mind of its construction, and scribbled something above the arch as shown on the upper left part of my sketch. Unfortunately, I could not complete the formation of the end points clearly in my mind enough to draw them.

When searching on the Internet, I happened to find a picture of the Golden Gates at Elvaston Castle in Derbyshire, England. The gates had been brought from the Palace of Versaillies by Charles Stanhope, the third Earl of Harrington, and moved to Derby. It was originally built in 1819.

I saw a definite similarity of this arch to my sketch, but perhaps there are many such arches in the U.K. To date, I have not been able to tie this particular arch to any previous life.

As I played on the castle walls, I peered deep down into what appeared to be a dungeon, though I had never known what one should look like. I confirmed what I had seen with Duncan. "They're usually quite deep into the ground," Duncan said. It was.

What I had seen were big, bold, gold Roman letters which now appeared as the numbers 1925. They took up my entire line of internal vision. Then the rest of the information started to come in. The stone walls of the castle were steel grey and rather large. I figured that they were about 18 inches wide by about 10 or 12 inches high.

Again, huge numbers appeared across my visual screen. The spirit world always gave me important information more than once. That doesn't mean that the year was actually on that archway. It was just a way of presenting that information. They must know how likely I am to lose such detail. I was now sure that the year was 1925. I was left to guess my age as being about twelve.

In the morning Duncan and I toured the neighborhood and took more pictures. As we walked, we found a church with an adjoining graveyard.

"Do you want to go in?" Duncan asked.

"Yes," I replied. I did.

Again, I found more tombstones of the same type, size and time period. I became quite excited. I thought Duncan would think that I was insane to be so thrilled about tombstones, but he seemed to overlook my exuberance.

An elderly man came from the direction of the church and said to me, "Have you been in the church?"

"No, I haven't," I replied.

"You should go in," he said. "It's beautiful in there."

"I'm sure it is," I offered, and he walked past me.

We looked a little further in the graveyard, and Duncan came across a grave marker that he felt belonged to his grandparents. He said that he had trouble locating it before.

Again, the old man came by me and beckoned me to go inside the church. "You have to go around, but the church is open. You should go in."

Duncan and I tried a couple of doors, but both were locked. We would have had to circle around the church to find the open door, and Duncan seemed anxious to get on our way.

He stopped to take photographs, and as he fussed with the camera and a new roll of film, I announced that I was going to go into the church.

"We'd better get going," he said. "We really don't have time."

I regretted that I was missing some karmic message that was to be given to me, but I didn't want to try Duncan's patience. I let it go. I felt sure that the man that beckoned me to go into the church was there for a reason. Twice he told me to go inside. I knew that he had been sent there for me.

Duncan had brought along a reference book, "NTC's Dictionary of the United Kingdom, The Most Practical Guide to British Language and Culture by Ewart James."

In it I found a black and white sketched picture of a castle that looked very much like the one that I had seen in my secondary vision. It appeared to have a dungeon deep below ground. It was called Caenarfon Castle which was also the name of a northern Welsh town with an administrative center of Gwynedd.

When doing research on this castle, however, I found that it is not made of the dark stone that I clearly remember. So, much more research is needed to find the castle that I lived in.

Chapter Twenty-Seven

Purbeck Stone

We were now headed to Dorset coast, which I had learned contained the chert stone that I had been looking for. Duncan was good at checking maps and knowing roads, times, distances, and areas in which to stay. He was a great travel companion as well as guide.

I continued to watch signs as we drove. I noted "Beacon Hill," "Quarry and Landfill," and "High View Hill Cemetery," all in Dorset.

I had learned that purbeck was an interchangeable word for some chert. A local gentleman confirmed with me that chert formations were in seven layers and came in the colors of black, red, green, brown, tan, grey and white.

In traveling, Duncan and I stumbled upon a Heritage Center in Lulworth that had many samples and descriptions of the rock in the area. The center was at a setting rich in exposed rock formations. It had beautiful cliffs, the English Channel, and a cove where a sailboat entered to moor for the night.

While the people at the center seemed unfamiliar with the term chert, I purchased a small booklet from them and found the information that I needed. I found that purbeck contained nodules of chert, which was a hard flint-like silica that fortified the rock.

Purbeck itself has five layers: a chalk limestone, green sandstone, wealden sandstone and clay, purbeck limestone and mud, and portland limestone.

We walked to the cliff's edge that overlooked the gorgeous water and harbor below. It was quite windy and cold that day. I had on a turtleneck, a light-weight shirt over that, and a dressy lightweight jacket.

When I got out of the car, I added another jacket. The wind picked up and it started to rain, so I put on another sweatshirt. I then put on a rain hat and another coat over everything else that I had on. Believe it or not, I was actually quite comfortable and did not feel cumbersome with all of those layers of clothing. I was also not at all cold.

After leaving the Heritage Center, Duncan was still determined to find a quarry for me for more information and samples. I saw a sign that said "Cement Works" in Westbury, and it was in that area that I began to see block that was very much like the cinderblock that I had been looking for.

"I'm going to have to find out what that block is," I told Duncan.

"Oh, I can tell you that," he said. "That's breeze block. It's man made, like cinderblock. There is no cinderblock here."

"How do you spell that?" I asked. His accent even eluded me at times.

"B-r-e-e-zed-e," he said. I had already learned that "zed" was "z" in the U.K.

Chapter Twenty-Eight

Sea Ports

We stayed in Swanage that evening at the Purbeck Hotel, which was right on the water. Duncan wanted us to have a water view, but I told him that wasn't really important. We spent little time in the room anyway.

In talking with the owner of the hotel, he had asked where we were going next. Duncan told him that I was looking for more Purbeck stone.

I said, "Actually, I'm looking for chert stone. Do you know what that is?"

"Why yes, I do," said the owner, and he immediately went to his back room and brought out a piece of highly polished chert stone that was to be used for decoration.

I was amazed to see a stone polished up to such beauty!

"Do you know anything about that stone?" I inquired.

"Well, it comes in seven layers, I know. There's a local bloke that knows all about it," he said, and proceeded to give us directions to find him. "There are also a couple of quarries near here too. Just follow the main road out of here and you'll find them."

I thanked him for his information.

We visited a quarry, but did not find chert stone. I was already delighted to have the information that I had.

Before leaving Swanage, we saw a steam train that ran through the outskirts of the city. We chased it so that Duncan could get a good camera shot.

Duncan took me to Poole Harbor, another beautiful place where sailboats came in and out from the sea. There we visited a Purbeck Pottery store where Duncan found a plate made of Purbeck stone that said Dorset Coast on the front. I bought the plate. It was a great souvenir from the area.

We took a ferryboat across to Bournemouth, where Duncan had lived and worked at one time. He certainly had an interesting and scenic home life based on what I had seen of his past.

We were back in the car again, and I was busily watching for signs and clues to my past lives. I was looking for quarries, brick makers, large steel tanks, and whatever else caught my attention.

I saw a sign for a brick kiln nursery in Bognor Regis and also a brick kiln farm. I also saw Deane & Dyball Construction, and figured they would probably know about making bricks.

Also in Bognor Regis I saw a sign that read Xavier House, which was probably attached to a private property wall. This sign was seen on a road going toward East Ashland and Bosham, and I noted this because of my innate interest in the name Xavier. This was a name that had come to me and which I identified as having belonged to my friend, Matt, from a former incarnation. I wondered if this was to tell me that he had lived there during a past life when I had known him.

Duncan and I stopped at a pub he had been to before. We parked on a road that was clearly marked, "This Road Floods Each Tide." Duncan explained that when the tide goes out, the road is usable. There is also a walking path across the entire bay that gets covered over each time the tide comes in.

He had parked on that road on one of his previous trips and was unaware of the tide situation. He had been sitting at the bar drinking when the pub owner told him that he had better move his car pretty quickly as the tide was coming in!

A tour of the neighborhood proved just that. As we walked down a street which had a slight decline, I noted that the doorways of the living quarters became shorter and the entrances higher. The last door was probably not more than four feet high and about two feet off of the pavement. A step led up to the doorway. It was obvious that the tide sometimes filled this street as well.

We stopped at a Saxon Church. According to Duncan, he believes the Saxon's ousted the Norman's from the area.

Our next stop was a place called Felpham. Duncan showed me a house, the second from the end of the street, where he had lived at one year of age. He had traveled there from India with his mother. She had lived in India, and his dad was stationed there while in the service. They married in India, had Duncan, and then moved to England. Duncan also showed me a nearby pub that his father had gone to, but a pub was never very hard to find in England.

Duncan and his mother had traveled from India to England by ship. The trip had taken a full month. I was able to see a picture of the ship in one of the restaurants of a place we stayed. I think it was the Royalist Inn, and the picture of the ship was hanging on the wall. The name of the ship was Durban Castle.

As we traveled the water's edge and stopped at each seaport, we ate fish and chips three nights in a row. The fish was always fresh Haddock, just caught in the sea and brought in by the fishermen from the fishing boats. It was excellent, and I didn't mind eating it day after day. The chips were actually French fries, and another common side dish was mushy peas. The peas were also fresh, mashed, and a bright shade of green. Duncan loved them, but I tired of them quickly.

Other typical English foods that Duncan loved were pork pie and steak and kidney pie. He certainly was able to get his fill of these early on in the trip. I wasn't even tempted, but was particularly cautious because of a breakout of hoof and mouth disease at the time of our trip. I was staying away from beef, and it was thought that some part of the pig was fed to the cows and I was skeptical of pork as well.

However, before the trip was over, I had consumed some bacon, beef liver, and ham. I might have suspected the beef liver as having made me ill, but Duncan ate the same thing that I did and finished what I didn't eat from my plate. He did not get sick.

We had dinner that evening in Arundel, overlooking the Arun River. Duncan told me that it was the fastest river in England. We were able to watch the tide come in as we ate our fish and chips.

Chapter Twenty-Nine

Homeward Bound

That evening we again passed through London and spent the night at Duncan's brother's house. We were kindly served a large cup of tea upon arrival, but the caffeine prevented both of us from getting sound sleep.

That night I saw more of the brick-making process in my mind's eye. The liquid mass was poured into a flat bed which was a large sheet with metal grate separators to make the brick forms. The brick was then baked in a large oven into a hardened state. I had never seen bricks being made in this lifetime, nor had I ever questioned the process of how they were made.

I was also contacted by some spiritual entity three times during the night, with a ringing sound in my ear, but I could not see anything and did not know what was intended in the message. However, I was aware that communication was trying to be made.

We were out of the house early the next morning and decided to stay closer to the airport in Epsom the last two nights of our trip. We had wanted to partake in a couple of walking tours and Duncan wanted me to see more of London.

One of the walking tours in which I was interested was called "Little Venice." The tour guides were all theatrical people and used this avenue for part-time employment. The tour guide we had was Emily, and she was a darling and quite demonstrative gal. She gave a history of the prominent Venetian homes of the area as well as of the canals. I was very interested in both, but primarily of the canals.

Some of the history included the creation of Little Venice by a man whose wife had died when they lived in Italy. He had wanted to leave all memories behind and had come to London to recreate a part of Venice.

The tour guide noted the pineapple symbol that was prominently displayed at the entranceway of some of the homes, and said that it stood for hospitality and welcome.

When she talked about the canals and the canal boats, she said that they were used specifically for the transporting of building materials and sometimes coal, but never for foods, wheat, or any produce. I expect that my father had transported his bricks on the canals of England.

I also learned that when the men worked the canals, they left their families for long periods of time. The wives hand painted roses on the sides of the canal boats, inside the doors, on watering cans, hand tools and everything they could find. They wanted to remind the men of the cottages they left behind.

I also saw homes with decorative plaques of very detailed flowers on both sides of some front doors. Some of the flowered plaques were colorfully painted, while others remained in a raised white state. That explains why, when taking a ceramic class many years ago, I thoroughly enjoyed the detailed hand painting of a couple of oval wall plaques that were filled with field flowers. I also recall coloring the imprinted flowers on paper napkins as a child.

With a nice break in between to enjoy coffee and pastries, we later took another walking tour called Ghost Walk. While one would think this would have been the most interesting to me, it was entertaining but not nearly as enlightening. The tour guide was not that diligent to see that his entire audience heard his words, but I did pick up some interesting pieces of information.

I learned that when there was a hanging in the center of town, the townsmen gathered in the nearby pubs to get good viewing seats of the event. They would arrive early, begin drinking, and by the time the hanging took place it became a gala event.

I also learned that as the person were hanged, if a good chap wanted to help his friend, he would walk by and pull on the friend's leg. This would tighten the noose and thereby expedite his death. Thus, the phrase, pulling my leg, came into existence.

The next day was Sunday, April 22, 2001. We were leaving England for home the following day. We drove to Richmond Hills, an area where Duncan used to live. It was a city on a high ridge overlooking the Thames River. We had coffee and tea in a plush café on the river's edge.

While I had been a confirmed coffee drinker and Duncan quite fond of his tea, we had reversed rolls at this point. I was now drinking tea with cream, which was something I had not done since I was a young woman. Duncan was drinking coffee.

The air had a slight chill, and we sat outside under gas heaters. I didn't think it would be possible to heat the outdoors so comfortably, but the heaters did well to keep us warm. There were both ceiling heaters under the overhang of the building and lantern-type heaters within the park setting.

I watched some of the entrees that were being served. One lady had poached eggs served on a high, fresh bed of spinach and English muffin.

We spent the rest of the day touring Hampton Court where Henry VIII once lived. It had also been inhabited by King William II and Queen Mary at another time, and the initials WM were prominently displayed in the stonework.

It was there that we found an English Maze. Duncan had me lead the way and to find our way out. One could virtually spend hours trying to make their way through, but having absolutely no sense of direction, I was able to find my way out with relative ease. I may not have a sense of direction, but logic must have prevailed.

By the time we got to Windsor Castle, it was raining again. It was not inviting to tour the grounds on foot, but I was certainly able to appreciate the vast size of the place.

We had dinner at a nearby pub and I met an East London Cockney man. Duncan had specifically wanted me to hear him speak, so he addressed him with a question.

"The words are twisted," the man said.

"They have a language all of their own," said Duncan. "I can't even make out some of the expressions he uses."

Here, at the last of our trip, I learned that the restroom was called a loo. I was also able to do a little souvenir shopping.

On the plane ride home, I saw another psychic vision of myself as a German lady with very full cheeks. I wore a dark dress with checks about two inches square, a white apron and cap. I was laughing, dancing, and singing German songs.

No wonder I had a German spirit guide, I thought. I had been told about Greta by a channelor; shortly after, she personally gave me a visit, showing up in God's circle of white light.

My mind drifted. Now I could see a small orange wooden boat on a very shallow body of water. The water appeared to be no more than a foot deep, and I could see ripples in the golden sand.

The trip was grand and perfectly timed. The weather in Michigan was just now beginning to get warm and the sun shone much brighter than it ever had in England. I loved the sun and soon could again appreciate the bright sunlight.

Chapter Thirty

Home At Last

My revelations did not stop upon returning home. They continued to come in with the freshness of the memories of England.

A surprising adjunct to my time in England was in seeing look-alike people with features and similarities to many of my friends and acquaintances here in the United States. It was most fascinating to find their almost duplicates in a faraway land. I wonder now if I was being told that those particular people were part of my soul family and had lived other lifetimes with me in England.

There was one other important thing that I noted to myself. It was a totally new and enriching experience. As I rode the subways and watched the people of many nationalities and cultures, I began to look at each person more intensely and sincerely. I felt a deep love for each and every one of them, regardless of their background or color. It was an unconditional love.

Another night at home, and I was being shown more of Charles' life. Since the year was 1925, and I had been reborn in 1944, I asked how long I had lived as Charles and what had happened to me.

Charles was at the castle where he lived, and I saw him walk through the large corridors. I could hear his accent and I wanted to call it a brogue. I could also hear his father speaking. He seemed quite harsh. He bellowed. I, as Charles, stayed clear of him.

The blocks of the castle were made of steel grey. Inside, I could see Charles' father walk within some vast chamber that went high into the air. From the ceiling hung chains that were joined at the bottom with a flat plate, about 5 to 6 feet in length and 12 inches in width.

Outside, I could see Charles in uniform. The streets were made of dark grey blocks, some with a deep red vein running through the stone. That would certainly pinpoint the area of England or Wales in which this Castle stood, since all of the buildings were constructed of the local stone. Charles was now about twenty years old.

Inside, but in open air, Charles stood somewhere (Is there someplace where names are not capitalized?) overlooking a castle wall. He stood on those grey blocks tipped with red at a place where headstones could be seen. At this point, a flash of something printed crossed my internal vision, and it was all in lower case.

The headstones had a depth of as much as 5 inches and a width of 2 feet. The tops of the markers were decorative. Charles stood there with a lady of his age, probably his girlfriend. She had red hair pulled back and tied at the neck. She was very attractive and he called her Gaye.

I had often thought to have a past-life regression performed, but here I was, able to produce my own. More revelations followed.

I now was getting information on Matt, my former friend and soul mate, whom I have named Xavier from a previous life. I had always presumed to have lived one or more lifetimes with him.

I was being told that he lived in a place called Grand Drake. His father lived in Sharon and his last name was Ryker. Two of my ornate shopping carts had been stolen while I was in Sharon. I wrote with my left hand then and was from Grand Duke. I lived in Ludwig on Tallscreet. I struggled to get all of the location names, as they were not coming in very clearly. I received information on a year of 1837 in relation to my life.

Another time I had a thought about my cousin Cheryl, and her last name from a previous life came to me as Snethcamp. I can recall her presence on a boat ride in England while growing up, and also knew that she had accompanied me on that walk path going to and from school. Her father, my uncle, was present at that steep, wet hillside. Was his last name Snethcamp at that time? I did not know.

It was now three weeks since returning from my trip to England, and the revelations have slowed down. A spiritual entity was with me last evening, but I let the playfulness of the message escape me. I knew that it was not serious and that I was being teased!

Chapter Thirty-One

Past-Life Synchronicities

Prior to the trip, my horoscope from one of my favorite writers had suggested that I would be meeting someone new in May and someone else in October. I was already planning on going to England, and the trip had been set for April.

After I read the horoscope, I jested with Gwenn, "See, that's why I have to take my trip to England with Duncan in April. I need to have that tie completed so that I can be open to meeting new people."

Since Duncan and I have been friends for many years, I was sure that we would continue to be as such. I also felt that the close union we would create during our trip would revert back to our previous quasi state after we returned.

It was now Friday night, and I was approaching a weekend that was relatively open to do whatever I chose to do. I had no commitments with anyone that I had to follow through on. I elected to meet a couple of friends at a popular gathering place that always had a great crowd, music, and many persons of our older age group.

The night proved to be entertaining, and I spent most of the evening dancing with a younger, pleasant gentleman. It was clear that he was only interested in dancing with me for the evening, and that made it comfortable. He was not looking for a further relationship. Throughout the evening my friends and I sat and talked with many men of our age group and were watched by others who were also interested in meeting us. It was a rare evening indeed in that we had much attention and interest all night.

Toward the end of the evening, Lorraine's eye found a man standing at a side bar rail watching the crowd and dance floor. She casually mentioned that he was a nice looking man. When I looked at him, I agreed, and said that he looked very much like a man I had met earlier that year. The former gentleman had encountered some unfortunate health setbacks and our friendship waned due to his needing time for recovery. That friendship was based on good conversation of similar interests.

When I had met him, he was completing rehabilitation from having broken some ribs, but I didn't know that. We had a long telephone conversation one evening, and he said that he would call again in a few days. I didn't hear from him, and I wondered if he was all right. I was quite sure that he was interested in calling again.

"Why would you think that?" commented my friend, Kristen. She was making a statement that men have been saying that they would call for years and didn't always follow through. "Why would you think there was something wrong?"

A couple of weeks later he did call and explained that he had fallen up his basement stairs, had broken some ribs, and had not been feeling well. It was then that I learned about his first fall and that he again had to refrain from activity. We did get together for a casual dinner late one afternoon, and again he said that he would call.

When he did not, I knew that something was wrong for the second time. I waited another week and then called, leaving a message in regard to my concern. I heard nothing back. Now I knew that there was something more seriously wrong.

I waited another week and called again, out of courtesy. This time he groggily answered and said, "Yes, I had a mild stroke." I could tell that his male ego had been shattered, his mortality was surely at the forefront of his mind, and he would have much bodily and emotional healing to do.

He was quite cordial. He said that he had received my first message, but that he just didn't know what to say. He therefore did not call me back. I told him that I understood, and we had more conversation until I felt he needed to rest and closed the call.

It was now pretty late in the evening and the band was playing their last piece. The nice-looking man at the side-rail bar now had moved himself directly in my view and asked if I would like to dance. I said yes, and we talked as we danced. Since it was the end of the evening, when the music stopped he said, "I would have liked to get to know you better. Would you be interested in meeting for a coffee tonight so we could talk for awhile?"

"Yes," I said. "That would be fine, except that I need to take Lorraine back to her car in Mt. Clemens. We met there and came here together."

"I'm going back toward that direction anyway, so you pick the place and I'll be there," he said.

I could only think of one place that was open twenty-four hours, so I suggested that we meet there. It was a relatively mutual spot for both of us, and I was interested in getting to know this man more. He was such a duplicate in looks to Ray, whom I had met earlier this year. In fact, the circumstances and the events that followed were almost identical.

I had only danced with Ray one time when Mary and I decided it was time to leave. She had to get up early for work the next morning, and it was a week-night dance. I was not working at the time, so the lateness was not as important to me. However, I had agreed that I would be willing to go whenever she was ready.

When I stood up to leave, the nice gentleman caught up with me and said, "Oh, are you leaving now? I had hoped to get to know you better. I hate to ask for your phone number so soon, but maybe we'll meet up again at another dance sometime."

I already knew from our discussion that neither of us went to the dances that often, so the chance of us meeting again would be highly improbable. "Oh, I don't mind," I quickly said. "I enjoyed meeting and talking with you."

He was appreciative of my response and obtained a pen and paper from someone nearby. My telephone number was provided, and having no more paper to write on, he made a point to verbally give me his full name and street address and the exact location of his home, even though it would be unlikely that I would remember it. It seemed important to him that I know exactly who he was and where he lived.

Now I was meeting John in much the same fashion as Ray. He looked like Ray, I danced with him only once before needing to leave, and he also wanted to give me a clear representation of who he was and where he lived, just as Ray had done. He scrambled to find a business card in his wallet, and when he could not find one, told me verbally his full name, street address, and the exact location of his home.

How similar the occurrences had been. He finally found one last business card in his wallet to give me, but the preceding events were hauntingly familiar from a look-alike man. Ray had expressed that he was a full German, and later that evening I found out that John was one hundred percent Polish.

Our evening went on until 4:30 a.m., so I was able to establish in my mind that he would be interesting and fun to know. He had a boat docked at a marina quite close to my home. We had similar interests, and he appeared to be quite a gentleman. I heard from him the following day, and he asked if I would like to come down to the marina. If not, he would come to my house. I invited him over, and we had a casual evening of drinks, conversation, and an occasional glance at the television programming when our conversation lapsed.

During that evening, with my being a New Age writer, much of our conversation centered on my experiences and his interest in the subject matter. I admitted to having the ability to see a symbolic representation of a person's inner self, and he was very much interested in my findings. I explained that I would no doubt have to have some quiet time before any such vision could come into my mind, but that I would seek out the information for him.

He expressed that he had recently lived foolishly, spending money on gambling, but that he had learned his lesson. He now jested that he could really use some cash; I was to find out when he would be getting money and the date that he would receive it. I said that I was in much the same state. I was looking for work now, but the job market was very tight and not promising. I had spent my money on living expenses while I continued to write. Then he added that I should find out when we would both be getting money.

The following day I had plans with Gwenn, and when I returned home, I found that he had called. His message stated that he hoped we could get together later on in the evening. A second night in a row was too much togetherness for me, and I felt a need to have my space. Even though Gwenn went home early enough that I could have entertained him, I elected not to return his call to the pager number left for me until it would be too late to see him.

After John had left my home the previous night, I made a conscientious effort to clear my mind in order to seek a symbolic vision of his character or soul. I received a blank screen. My mind was still fairly cluttered with crisscrossing thoughts of recent events, but I worked on clearing it again. A blank screen presented itself to me again, and I surmised that I needed to have a clearer mind and drifted off to sleep.

In the morning I reasoned that I was given the blank screen because I was not to learn the symbolic likeness of him just yet. There was something else that I needed to learn before I would be given this information. I then wondered about the similarities between Ray and John and if it was something that pertained to them.

Having been given little information other than the realization of events of synchronicity, I consulted the tarot cards for answers for both John and myself in regard to money. First I read the cards for him. The tarot appeared to want to give me four cards instead of the usual three for a yes or no question, so I laid out four cards. His reading alluded to lessons learned, the potential for creative ability, and the likelihood of a monetary gain. I was sure John would be pleased to hear that.

Twice during the night before, I also received information in regard to a type of invention. The spirit world knows me well, and when they want to make a point, the same information is presented to me twice. Otherwise, I might overlook it.

The invention was to be a computerized chip for an electronic fondue. The information was bazaar in itself, and it was certainly unclear as to what this computer chip was to do that an electronic fondue could not already accomplish.

I wasn't sure if the message was intended for John. It could easily have been meant for someone else that I had been talking to the same evening. I would present the information to him regardless, being the messenger that I was intended to be.

When I asked the tarot about my obtaining a job soon to satisfy my own monetary needs, my fortune was not to be as lucky. There were things that I needed to learn, and I was to be given the solitude of that time in order to discover them.

I was not exactly elated with this projection. I knew that I needed cash income and fairly soon. My funds were rapidly dwindling, and I had heavy expenditures that I still wanted to make. I had some extensive cement work I wanted done which was to include a replacement patio, and I fully intended to purchase an expensive sewing machine which was going on sale in a couple of weeks.

My cards did say, however, that although I was to learn to live more prudently, that did not mean that I should eliminate the expenditure of those things that I felt were appropriate. To me that meant that I should still spend the money for those things I felt fitting for my cause. The sewing machine was one of them.

Each time thoughts of John came to mind throughout the day, I pictured a different face. I would realize that I was picturing another face, with the voice I heard in my head, and would shake it out of my mind. Later, thoughts of him would return, and I would again see someone else's face. Who was I seeing? Who did this man remind me of that I was seeing in my mind's eye?

I couldn't place him. Now I couldn't see the face clearly enough to determine who that might be, but with thought I could clearly see John's real face because it was so much like Ray's. The face did not match the voice I heard in my head.

Late that evening, I returned John's call to his pager. Moments later the phone rang. I answered the call to find that it was an operator asking if I would accept a collect call from him. I made the operator repeat the information, as I was trying to figure out why I was receiving a collect call, and was it really from him? I agreed to accept the charges. I thought that something must be wrong; perhaps he needed help and was unable to reach anyone else that he knew.

The voice on the other end of the line was not distressed, but I pressed for information. "Is something wrong? Why are you calling collect?" I asked.

"You paged me, didn't you?" he said.

"Yes, I did, but is something wrong?"

"No," he said. "I've just had a very bad day. I dropped my cell phone in the lake, and it has gone down hill from there."

Annoyed that he had called me collect for this information, I said, "Is there a number where I can call you back? I'm sure I'm paying a premium for this call."

"I'm not that far from you," he said. "What I need is a dip in a hot tub. I've had quite a day." He had seen the hot tub at my house and was pressing for an invite.

"Not tonight," I assured him. He pressed a little more, but I was solidly holding my ground. I minimized our discussion and was unwilling to expound on any psychic information that I had obtained for him. I was not willing to entertain casual dialogue on my reluctantly offered dime. We ended the conversation pleasantly.

That evening, I again sought information in regard to John's symbolic representation. I found alternate images of a man crawling out of a manhole, the man whose face

I see in my mind's eye instead of his, and a black widow spider also crawling out of this hole. Which was he, I questioned in my mind.

I let it go, and as always, the same alternate visions returned until I was convinced it was what I was meant to see. Neither element felt comfortable to me. Was this a warning to me? Was this the first harmful person I was to encounter? The first bad image I was ever to receive? And why? What did it mean? Was the black widow spider warning me of the danger of this man? This man who was trying to bring himself back to a good life and was climbing out of this hole?

It was now Monday morning, and I reflected upon this vision. I would call Gwenn for more information on the visual description and intricacies of black widow spiders. She was always able to expound on the information that I needed. I continued to see the other man's face instead of John's. His face was much more appealing. Why was I seeing another face? And whose face was it? Again I tried to identify the face to someone that I knew, but I still could not place who that might be.

I looked up black widow spider in the dictionary. The definition seemed incomplete and stated that it was a New World spider, often using a deadly venom. The female was black and had red markings on its body indicating that it ate its mate.

Now I knew. Synchronicities. All of the details were now coming to me. This was the additional information that I needed to know to solve the mystery of what has haunted me for all of these years. Portions of conversation were coming back to me from my first and second meetings with John.

John had two children, a boy and a girl, as did I. There were other similarities in our lives as well, but not necessarily the synchronous things I needed to reveal his identity. His son was a successful doctor of psychiatry; his daughter had done well in advertising. He was proud of both of his children, but especially his son, revealing his special accomplishments with a misfortunate hardship. His son had been born with an eye affliction. He was not blind, but had a spasmodic condition of blinking, or fluttering of the eye, with which he had learned to live.

Now I knew who the other face was and who John was in a previous life. He was the deadly black widow spider of my psyche. It was this man, the man of the other face, who had tormented my friend in the insane asylum. He was the doctor who had tortured my visionary friend to his death in that sterile room of the white block building. John, the man of the other face, now has a son with an eye affliction. It was he who provoked the feelings that haunted me for years.

My thoughts were telling me that the torture that killed my friend was through the eye, since he was the disbelieved visionary. Now John has had to suffer the pain of his son's affliction in this life for his mistreatment of someone else in a previous life.

John was the psychiatrist of the past, and the synchronicity of the son now being the psychiatrist with the eye affliction was the connection I needed to make to pull the loose ends together.

John, a tool and die maker in this life, was also to give me a clue, but its relative unimportance did not help me tie this information together. My father was a tool and die maker in this life.

Now I needed to know if John would be a good friend for me in this lifetime. Did I see him crawling out of the manhole representing that he was coming out of the blackness of his past? Was he now going to be a good person? Would he finally be relieved of his sin? Or will the deadly black widow spider continue to lurk nearby him? I would soon learn and make my judgment.

I told Gwenn about my newly acquired disclosure. She agreed that John's son is my friend of my former life, since people are born into new lives carrying with them an affliction from a past-life encounter.

I wondered if I had acquired the knowledge of what I needed to learn to now get a job, so I asked. The answer was no; I had not. I had completely forgotten that there was a lesson for me in this consequence as well.

In that past life, I had stood by my friend knowing that he was being tortured and had done nothing to stop it. I had only shown up later to comfort him. I must have been afraid of the authority in that lifetime and did not speak up. I did not use the *power* that I had within me.

I was weak in character, and the realization of failing him, resulting in his tortured death, followed me into this life. That is the unseen horror that I feel when I see white cinderblock buildings. I must now give deep thought as to whether I have learned that lesson in this lifetime or if I still needed to atone for my sin and pay my karmic debt.

Chapter Thirty-Two

Fragments of My Lives

During my sleep, I received more information in regard to a former life. The information came more toward morning and I was in a dreamlike state. I questioned the validity of some of the information because of it, and could almost relate it to current events of my life. However, some of it I knew was definitely psychic information, and I note it here.

One of my two son's names was Jason, and he was planning on going to a university for higher learning. I would guess his age to be about 16 or 17 at that time. Some adult in the room, not related, was influencing him about being interested in sports.

Then I heard a black man's voice say, "Our broken sister, Mary Bea, plays in-field." I wasn't sure how this was to tie in, but noted it. This was later followed by input of my husband's name being Bud.

I asked Gwenn about colleges in those days and if they even existed. "Yes, they were called universities."

Then I asked her if baseball was a sport then. Again, she had the information that I needed. "Yes, baseball was an American sport invented by Abner Doubleday." I confirmed that he played baseball as early as 1839 with the rules being officially defined in 1845. How she knew all of this information was just amazing to me.

I now had enough information to start piecing together

the many fragments of my lives that I had learned. I began to chart them with the years given me and to put them together with my other findings.

I was sure that the chart would evolve as I learned more. The years that I knew for sure were 1837 from my life with Xavier; 1860 from Ralph, my spirit guide, when I failed my visionary friend's needs in the insane asylum; 1925, from the clearly given information about Charles, and 1944, the year of my current life's birth. This chart includes several lives.

I have learned that my same mother, father and grandmother from this life existed in my life in England. My much earlier vision of many years ago consisted of two tombstones located close together, and another a great distance from the two. I am speculating that the two together belong to my mother and father, and the one in the distance belongs to my grandmother. These were important people in my current life. These lives were from the 1800's.

My uncle was also present in that lifetime, even though he was not blood related to me in my current life. My cousin, his daughter, was a soul mate as well, but I found her present only in walking with me along the stone wall of the path from home to school, and on the canal boat ride.

I have spent countless hours on the Internet researching the information that was provided, but unfortunately do not have many first and last names to work with. I also checked a city and road map from a rental car agency. Street names and city names were not found in the vicinities in which I searched, but perhaps do exist in some other areas.

I suspect that the day I received the information on the street name of Tallscreet in Ludwig and a city name of Sharon were attempts of communication in which I only got part and completed each word with a familiar sound. Ludwig could have been Lerwick, Ludford, Ludlow, Ludwell or even London. Sharon could have been Sharow, Charing and so on. Unless there is a specific spelling provided, or a specific year, there is room for misinterpretation.

Interestingly enough, there is a place called Sole Street (Tallscreet) not far from Charing (Sharon), bordering the North Downs in Kent, England. Charing, where I may have lived, is right off of M20 out of London, and Sole Street is quite close, and in a straight line east. In addition, this seems to be the only area in England where cities or towns have names with the word street in them. In the message, I assumed that what I was hearing as Tallscreet or Tallstreet was the street name in the city of what I heard as Ludwig; it did not occur to me that it might be a town. I can't place Ludwig anywhere on the map, but London is certainly appropriate.

When trying to link the names Xavier and Ryker together as a first and last name, the result was nil. One of my author friends, also psychic, said to me, "If you're like me, you get a first name from one lifetime and a last name from another. Then when you assume you have a full name and try to find that person, the name does not exist." I tend to agree with her findings.

In trying to trace George, Hank and Diane Smede, I was able to find family records for George Henry Smedes with alternate spellings of Smeed and Smeedes, for the same record, in both London and Kent, England, and in the correct time period. Even more curious was a listing for a Mary Smead in Cheriton, Kent, England—remembering the letters c-h-e-r-i-t given me psychically. I will probably never really know my direct ties to these people. The name Diane was not traceable at all, but many times women's names were not registered.

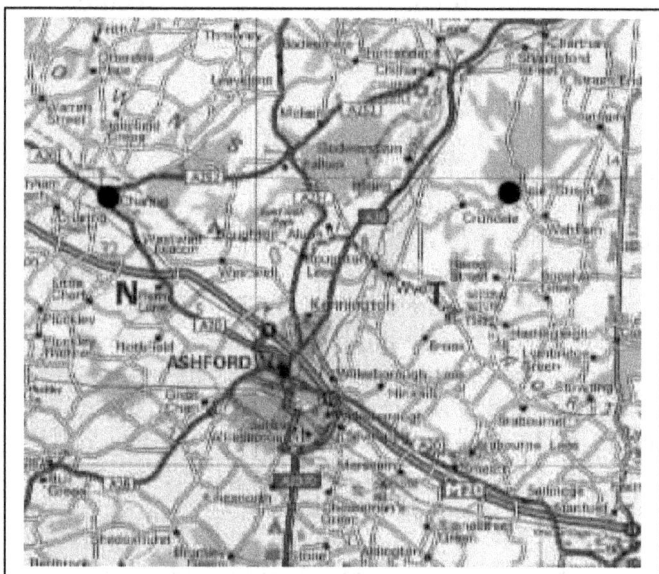

While trying to find areas in England that contained the dark grey stone of the castle where Charles lived, it occurred to me that I had forced the thought that it should be in England; yet much of the information provided me told me that it might be Ireland or even Scotland. The dark stone, the brogue accent, the girl with the red hair, and the grave markers with decorative tops were all specific clues given me.

"You'd be more likely to see those decorative tombstones in Ireland than England," commented Duncan. My search continues.

I continually struggle to plug all of the holes that are somewhere within the caverns of my mind and within the past-lives chart where there are no explanations. With the many answers that I found on my journey, I was also presented with that many more questions. I am so aware that the memory need only be piqued with some mere reminder to bring forth more information. One must just find the key to open that door.

I am fortunate to have had the opportunity to discover fragments of my past lives and to have experienced the many revelations that I had in regard to those memories. I would never have expected to experience such revelations. While some were entirely new, as my life as Charles and the German lady, each were an experience quite inexplicable by any other means.

Even though Gwenn tried to prepare me for a true pilgrimage, I was totally unaware of the information that would follow. I found a childhood life near the canals of England, the actual hillside I had fearfully slid down as a youngster, and the path that I took as I walked to school. All of these things became live memories from what I had thought were childhood dreams.

I also learned why my favorite toy as a child was a set of red building bricks made of wood and why I liked to color the flowers on my mother's white paper napkins. How else would I ever have tied my love of the bricks to my past father's livelihood or my love of painting to my past mother's painting in that era?

Most of all, I have finally resolved the mystery of my unyielding emotions when seeing white cinderblock buildings. Although I did not find the building in England that provoked my years of searching for explanations, I was later given the opportunity to meet the man who could unknowingly convey the answers.

Past-Lives Chart

Perhaps it is the rudimentary way in which one must retreat in order to have the visions of the past come forward, or the many shallow trances one must perform in order to look inside ones' own depth that leave one feeling unsettled about self regression.

Ellen Marie Blend

Year(s)	Relationship	Past Life Name
1837	Self	
1837	Self	
1837	Soul Mate	*Xavier*
1837	Soul Mate's Father	Last name *Ryker*
1847 - 1897		
1752	Possible Ancestor	Mary Smead
	Mother	*Diane*
1845	Father	George Henry Smede
1859	Father	*George* Henry *Smede*
1861	Self	
	Grandmother	
1864	Self	
	Uncle	
	Father	
1863	Brother	Henry (*Hank*) John Smede
	Brother	Married Ann Rains 1876
1856	Ann Rains	Married Brother Hank 1876
1879	Brother's Son	George Smeed
	Cemetery near hill	**Banbury, England**
	Mother	
	Brother	
	Self	
	Self	
	Uncle	Last name *Snethcamp*

Notes: *Italicized* years and names were given in psychic meditation or by a channelor.
Bolded years and facts are from recorded information.

Birth Record	Comments
	Tallscreet (Sole Street) in Ludwig (London)
	Lived in Grand Duke; age about 20
No record	Lived in Grand Drake
No record	Lived in Sharon (Charing)
The transporting of bricks via canals peaked in the 1800's.	
Cheriton, Kent, England	Married Thomas Pitcher 1773
No record	
Spitafields Christ Church, Stepney, London, England	Father John; Mother Amelia; No record of spouse
	Father transported bricks via canals
	Age 2 - 3 Fear of mother not coming back
	Held me while mother went in boat w/father
	Age 5 - 7 Canal Boat Ride (River Cherwell?)
	Coaxed me to slide down steep hill
	Father made red bricks; used cart with name *Smede & Son*
Spitafields Christ Church, Stepney, London, England	
Marriage:	Ospringe, Kent, England
Marriage:	Ospringe, Kent, England
Marriage:	Ospringe, Kent, England
	Southam Road Evalangical Church
	Age 9 - 10 Helped father in stable
	Age 4 - 5 Childhood fear under bed
	Age 5 - 7 Called mother Mama
No record	

Year(s)	Relationship	Past Life Name
1833	Self	Ann Smede
1838	Self	Ann Smede
1855	Self	Nottingham, England
1860	Self	Ann Smede
1860	Self	Ann Smede
1860	Psychiatrist	
1860	Aide in Hospital	*Gregory*
1860	Patient	*Thomas*
1833		Ann Raine Smede
		Mother
		Aunt
		Self
	Self	
		Bud
		Jason
		?
1913	Self	*Charles*
1925	Self	*Charles*
1925		
1932	Friend	*Gaye*
1932	Self	*Charles*
1943	Self	Male
1943	Self	Male
1943	Self	Male
1913 - 1986	Mother this life	Edith Hellebuyck/LeDuc
1901 - 1961	Father this life	Nicholas Radensik
1944	Self	Ellen Blend

Notes: *Italicized* years and names were given in psychic meditation or by a channelor.
Bolded years are from recorded information.

Birth Record	Comments
	Possible birth year
	Walk path to/from school by Mapperly Hospital
Nottingham, England	Possible nursing school Mapperly Hospital
	Age 25-35 Nurse in psychiatric hospital
	Found tortured friend dead in sterile room
	At insane asylum/hospital
	At insane asylum/hospital
	Visionary friend in insane asylum
Married Thomas Raine	Middridge, Durham, England
	Waited in front of apartment building for father
	Waited in front of apartment building for father
	Age 7-8 Waited in front of apartment building
	Age 30-35 Inside of home with candle light
	Husband's name
	Son's name, age 16-17
	Other son, no name provided
	Baseball founded 1839; officially defined 1845
	Possible birth year
	Age 12 playing on castle walls
	Castle: steel grey stone with red vein
	Red-haired lady friend with Charles
	At castle, in uniform, with Gaye
	Age 30, being lowered into large tank or well
	Seen at war on hillside with rifle
	Shot through helmet and died
	Born in Detroit, Michigan
	Born in Dunlo, Pennsylvania
	Born to Edith and Nicholas Radensik

www.familysearch.org